The Mystical Power of
Person-Centred Therapy

Dedication

In memory of George Aubrey Lyward, whose genius, vulnerability and practical mysticism unlocked the prison of contractual living for so many.

The Mystical Power of Person-Centred Therapy
Hope Beyond Despair

BRIAN THORNE

Emeritus Professor and Director of the Centre for Counselling Studies,
University of East Anglia, Norwich

W

WHURR PUBLISHERS
LONDON AND PHILADELPHIA

First published 2002 by
Whurr Publishers Ltd
19b Compton Terrace, London N1 2UN, England and
325 Chestnut Street, Philadelphia PA 19106, USA

Reprinted 2002 and 2003

British Library Cataloguing in Publication Data

A catalogue record for this book is available from the British
Library.

ISBN 1 86156 328 0

Printed and bound in the UK by Athenaeum Press Limited,
Gateshead, Tyne & Wear.

Contents

Acknowledgements

There are many in the international community of person-centred scholars and therapists who have contributed to this book through their understanding and their own spiritual quests. I am particularly indebted to the late Dr Maria Bowen and, among my European colleagues, to Professor Mia Leijssen, Professor Martin van Kalmthout and Professor Peter Schmid for their writings and generosity of spirit.

As always, the unfailing support of the secretarial staff at the University Counselling Service of the University of East Anglia has been crucially important to me. Most especially I wish to express my thanks to Paula Middleton whose efficiency and creativity have won my unbounded admiration. I have been singularly blessed to have had the enthusiastic help of so skilled an assistant at every stage of the book's evolution.

Prologue

This book is a mixture of diary and reflection. It begins in June 2000 when, like many others, I was grieving for the loss of a dear colleague who had died after collapsing during a counselling session. It ends in September 2001 only a few days after the suicidal terrorist attacks on the World Trade Centre and the Pentagon. Not surprisingly, perhaps, a book framed between these two events is not concerned with minor issues. On the contrary, at the risk of seeming grandiose in the extreme, I have attempted to explore why, for me, the practice of person-centred therapy is a profound spiritual discipline which offers a powerful message to the world at a period of terrifying uncertainty.

I am somewhat unusual, I know, in combining my work as a person-centred therapist with a commitment to the spiritual tradition of an institutional church. For some of my professional colleagues this dual allegiance is difficult to understand or to accept while there are many of my co-religionists who consider me to be dangerously heretical and an enemy of the true Faith. Perhaps it is this often somewhat lonely position which has contributed to my growing conviction that the theory and practice of person-centred therapy have within them the promise of a hope which lies beyond our current despair. From my own experience both as a person-centred therapist and as a Christian who often feels in exile, I have concluded that Carl Rogers was right when he stated that he had 'underestimated the importance of this mystical, spiritual dimension' which his therapeutic experience had revealed to him in the later years of his life.

This book takes Rogers' statement with the utmost seriousness and attempts to spell out its implications not only for the practice of therapy and the training of therapists but also for understanding and addressing the seemingly intractable conflicts which currently hold the world to ransom. Such an undertaking has, at times, resulted in crippling self-doubt and I have hesitated to put such reflections in the public domain. I do not, after all, wish to place my professional reputation in complete jeopardy and I do not lightly

risk the accusations of being foolishly naïve, outrageously arrogant or profes-
sionally unethical. I realize that what I have written makes me vulnerable to
all three judgements and probably others which are equally condemnatory.
There is, however, in me, to use recent person-centred terminology, a family
of configurations all of which, as I move gradually off the professional stage,
demand to be heard. The therapist, the 'secular priest', the prophet, the
linguist, the theologian, the recluse, the dramatist, the belletrist, the lover,
the professor have all made their contribution to the chapters which follow
and I can only hold my breath and trust that there will be those among my
readers who can find at least some crumbs of nourishment for their own
intermittent battle with despair and meaninglessness.

Last night, I was telephoned unexpectedly by Dr Natalie Rogers, Carl's
daughter. More than she will ever know, Natalie encouraged me to believe
that I have not perhaps completely taken leave of my senses. She assured me
that she regarded my study of her father, first published in 1992, to be an
accurate portrayal of the man she knew so well (Thorne 1992). In that book I
made no secret of my belief that there was a covert spiritual thread in Rogers'
work from the outset and that history would show him to be one of the major
influences on the spiritual evolution of twenty-first century humanity. This
present volume seeks to develop this thesis in the light of my own life and
experience as a person-centred therapist. Natalie's phone call persuades me,
on the best authority, that my perception of her father has validity and that to
speak of the mystical power of person-centred therapy is to use a language
with which, in the last years of his life, he was already growing familiar.

CHAPTER 1

Person-centred therapy since Carl Rogers

As often in the past, I begin the writing of a book seated in a railway carriage. Within a few feet of me a hard-faced woman is jabbering into a mobile phone, a younger one is peering wearily at the screen of her laptop. Opposite me a man with furrowed brow is 'wired up' to something or other and is apparently listening to music – or is it to a distance learning programme on some aspect of the insurance industry to which the folder in front of him indicates his allegiance? Yesterday my daily newspaper contained a quotation from Max Frisch which cynically reflected that the achievement of technology is to arrange life so that we do not have to experience it. Intermittently I feel old and wonder if my escalating disenchantment with much that passes for 'progress' is simply a reflection of an incapacity to adjust to a changing culture or a fear that the reference points that have given some coherence to my own life are about to vanish completely. And yet I know that these encapsulated people around me bear a family resemblance to many clients who have sat with me in recent years and lamented their loss of fun, their lack of intimacy and their abject capitulation to a drivenness which has made the world of work for them a joyless treadmill. I am also aware that the daily wonders of information technology (and their rapid obsolescence) are more the outcome of commercial greed and competitiveness than of altruistic human inventiveness. I am suddenly reminded of my decision more than 30 years ago never to drive a car again after five of my friends had been killed in road accidents within a year and I had tumbled to the fact that this lethal machine not only killed countless human beings but also had the potential to poison the whole earth. Everything that has happened since has served to reinforce that gloomy prediction. I have sometimes fantasized that the end of the world, or at least the end of humanity, will take the form of a global gridlocked asphyxiation and to this picture I must now add the sound effects of the last gurglings of a wired-up species, which talks and communicates incessantly but knows no sustaining communion and senses but fails to confront the void beyond the words.

1

Am I a seer, or simply a doom-monger? Often I do not know but at least I try to stay close to the 'flow or experience' within me and to affirm the basic tenets of the therapeutic tradition to which I have devoted the best part of my professional life. As a person-centred therapist, I remain committed to trusting my own experience and to believing that if I can be truly self-acceptant, I may be able to offer to others the unconditional acceptance and the empathic understanding which they need for their flourishing. There is more. I do not wish to deny the yearning that I myself have for unconditional acceptance and the accompanying realization that, however significant and essential the loving affirmation of others is for me, it can never be quite enough to release me completely from the inner loneliness which always threatens to engulf me in meaninglessness. I remember Abraham Maslow's distress when, near the end of his life, he was forced to acknowledge that there were those who had had all their basic needs satisfied and had received plenty of applause and appreciation but who, looking out on the world and society, felt utterly hopeless in the face of the shambles which they perceived. As he realized that a central plank of his theory of the hierarchy of needs was disintegrating, Maslow declared himself to be 'more of a missionary than ever' as he attempted to discover what kept the self-actualizing motivation alive in some while others, despite all the affirmation they received, metaphorically died within (Frick 2000: 140–41).

By rights, I ought not to be on this train at all. I should be in my university presiding over the final stages of the examination process which will see another cohort of person-centred therapists released into the world. Of all days, this is the day when the work ethic requires that I be at my post fulfilling my obligations as an academic whose life is increasingly infected by the demands of teaching quality control and research assessments. Death, however, has intervened and restored a sense of perspective and a proper concern for priorities. Death has a habit of restoring balance to life and of revealing the triviality of our obsessional preoccupations. Serious illness often has the same beneficial effect. Perhaps that is why my greatest fear about the genome project is not that our genes will be patented – horrific as that is – but that by promising physical immortality it will make it even more difficult for us to endow life with meaning.

Instead of sitting in an examiners' meeting, I am on my way to the funeral of a dear friend and colleague. Mary Kilborn (1943-2000) was a prominent person-centred therapist, supervisor and trainer, whose life and work brought hope to many. She died following a brain haemorrhage which tragically occurred during a counselling session. She was not old and her premature death has brought intense grief and desolation to her family, her friends, her colleagues, her clients, her supervisees and her trainees. I am among those who mourn profoundly her passing. And yet, as I travel to her funeral, I experience a sense of freedom and release. It is as if I am liberated to live, however briefly, in a world immeasurably greater than that to which my normal day-to-day existence usually gives access. Since her death a week ago it is as if I have been living outside time and space and that many of Mary's friends whom I have encountered in my grief and shock have been living there, too.

When a person dies in their prime, the questions of meaning and purpose cannot be evaded and the evaluation of a human life has to take place without the reflective distance which old age or a lengthy retirement can provide. As, 24 hours later, I resume the writing of this book, I am still caught up in the experience of Mary's funeral and my head is full of conversations with several of the people who turned out in their hundreds to pay their final respects to a person who had so enriched their lives. The themes of those conversations were strikingly similar. Mary, it seemed, was experienced as a person for whom her professional life and activity were a central part of her spiritual search. Her quest for self-acceptance informed and inspired her acceptance of others and gave to them a framework for meaning and hope. Her conviction that she was a person of infinite worth, despite seeming evidence to the contrary and despite her own, at times, stubborn resistance to such a self-conceptualization, proved powerfully infectious. It clearly enabled her to extend herself in her work with clients and to offer an accompaniment of committed compassion and understanding which often exceeded by far what might normally be expected of a therapist. Her preparedness to take risks and to run the danger of being accused of over-involvement (a favourite term of abuse employed by therapists who wish to legitimize their own fear of relationship) communicated to many of her most wounded clients a sense of their inherent worth which no amount of clever talk or analytical acuity could have achieved. The effect on a human life of being validated in this way, after perhaps years of rejection, indifference or abuse is, of course, transformational. It conveys a message that goes to the heart of a person's being and bypasses entirely the need to perform or to win approval. It is this conferring of existential value which clearly characterized much of Mary's work and which, I would suggest, places person-centred therapy, at its best, firmly in the arena of spiritual and transcendental activity. Such a claim can perhaps be most readily substantiated by focusing for a moment on the famous core conditions in person-centred therapy which in themselves enshrine a way of being with self and with others which has the profoundest implications for the understanding of human nature and of human destiny.

The person-centred therapist is charged with the awesome task of becoming fully human and the core conditions are the applied practice of that task. It is as if the work of the professional therapist in the person-centred tradition constitutes a challenge of an existential and spiritual order under the deceptive guise of a professional identity. I often say to trainees that by determining to become person-centred therapists they have accepted the responsibility of furthering their own growth towards full humanity as a professional obligation. The core conditions, often so summarily dismissed or even sometimes affirmed by those who have no true understanding of them, are, in fact, an invitation to embrace a way of being which demands not less than everything. The commitment to constant self-exploration and self-aware-ness which is the prerequisite for the genuine expression of the self (congru-ence), the dedication to the expressed understanding of the other's world (empathy) and the ability willingly to accept unconditionally the other person in all his or her kaleidoscopic uniqueness (unconditional positive regard) – this is the disciplined agenda of a lifetime. It can only be undertaken by someone who has a profound faith in the infinite worth of the human person, including himself or herself, despite the often considerable challenges to such a faith from the destructive behaviour and denigration of persons by which our culture is frequently characterized and in which we are all implicated. As I listened to the mourners after Mary's funeral their testimony was clear and unequivocal. For them, Mary inspired and healed not because she was perfect but because she had glimpsed the glory of her own being and conveyed to others that they shared with her a common inheritance. Within the struggle and the anguish of the therapeutic relationship she had found the means of confirming the infinite value of the human person and in so doing she had conferred meaning on herself and others. What is more, she had revealed a resourcefulness and connectedness within the cosmos which is both exempli-fied and illuminated by the experience of relational depth made possible by the disciplined offering of the core conditions.

Carl Rogers would have understood the experience of the mourners at Mary's funeral. In the years following his own wife's death he dared, it would seem, to enter ever more deeply into relationships with both clients and friends and began to employ language which he would have assiduously eschewed in earlier years. Both in groups and in one-to-one relationships he claimed to experience phenomena for which the only available language included such words as 'spiritual', 'mystical' and 'transcendent'. Rogers spoke of a quality of presence in his own being – the outcome of many years disciplined cultivation of the core conditions – which was in itself healing and which gave access to 'something larger' than the sum of the persons present. He used the language of connectedness and even dared to entertain notions of a continuing sense of identity beyond death (Rogers 1980: 92, 129). The Rogers of this post-1979 period was giving expression to reflec-tions which were a far cry from the cautious utterances of the empirical scientist of earlier years. And yet for him, as always, they were anchored in experience and were the outcome of his unswerving fidelity to his personal apprehension of reality even when, as in this case, such fidelity involved the rethinking or even a radical revision of a previous position.

In the years since Rogers' death in 1987, there has undoubtedly been a deep ambivalence in the international person-centred community to his late engagement with issues of spirituality and mystical experience. There is even some evidence that Rogers himself in the years immediately preceding his death was less inclined to explore such terrain, although there is also no doubt that he continued to be increasingly intrepid in the conduct of his personal relationships. Be that as it may, it is certainly the case that there are currently many person-centred practitioners who find Rogers' late foray into the spiritual arena as embarrassing, if not more so, than his passionate commitment to the person of Jesus Christ as a young man and his subsequent pursuit of theological training. I do not share that embarrassment: on the contrary, together with many of my British and other European colleagues, I am persuaded that it is in the later work of Carl Rogers that we find the most powerful pointers to where the cutting edge of the approach is likely to be found in the new millennium. I have little doubt that many of the mourners at Mary's funeral would share that conviction and that their belief would be anchored, as it was for Rogers, in their experience of person-centred therapy where the therapist has embodied the core conditions as a way of being in the world – a response, that is, to a spiritual imperative and not the implementation of a misunderstood therapeutic technique.

Carl Rogers had much in common with Elizabeth Kübler-Ross, the distinguished and radically innovative physician whose groundbreaking work with the terminally ill shot her to world fame in the 1970s. Words from her last book, written as she approached her own death, were read at Mary's funeral and in some ways they serve as an appropriate commentary not only on her own life but on Mary's too and on the life of Carl Rogers. They also convey in the most concise way possible why it is that person-centred therapy can claim to be not only an empirically researched therapeutic approach but also a mystical path for therapist and client which requires no dogma, no guru and no spiritual exercises. All that is required is a preparedness for two people to meet at relational depth and for one to be thoroughly schooled in the practice of offering the core conditions to herself and to the other who seeks her help. Elizabeth Kübler-Ross put it this way: 'The sole purpose of life is to grow. The ultimate lesson is learning how to love and be loved unconditionally' (Kübler-Ross 1997: 287). It is my experience that person-centred therapy at its best reveals and reinforces for both client and counsellor that the 'sole purpose of life is to grow' and then proceeds to make possible the 'ultimate lesson' through its capacity to give access to 'something larger' than the relationship itself which remains nonetheless the primary channel for such enhanced resourcefulness.

Those in the person-centred world who find most difficulty with such language and with the spiritual gloss on Rogers' work are by no means necessarily those who have an antipathy to religion or religious institutions. There is a growing recognition that religion and spirituality are not by definition connected and the very word 'spiritual' is commonly used by those who wish to affirm their belief in an overarching reality which points to the interconnectedness of the created order and to a perception of the human being as essentially mysterious and not ultimately definable in biological, psychological or sociological terms. There are prominent person-centred practitioners – including my close colleague, Dave Mearns at the University of Strathclyde (Mearns and Thorne 1988, 1999, 2000) – who declare themselves atheist or agnostic but who acknowledge the reality of the phenomena which spiritual language attempts to describe and explore. They are more likely to use existential terminology but they do not doubt that the experience of relational depth opens up channels for understanding and profound connectedness which can transform a person's sense of self and engender new hope and meaning. What matters is not so much the use of 'spiritual' or 'existential' language as the recognition that trusting in the process of person-centred therapy can lead to the experience of a relational encounter which is transformational because it touches the essential core of the personality. In some ways both languages are attempting to do justice to a level and quality of experiencing which in former times might have evoked the language of miracles.

Those who find most difficulty with the spiritual and mystical claims of person-centred therapy are often those who are openly and unashamedly pragmatic and do not wish to see the approach banished to the margins of the therapeutic mainstream because it has been deemed woolly-minded, empirically shaky or even suspiciously 'new-agey' and alternative. The current obsessional concern with evidence-based practice, short-term efficacy and measurable outcomes has led to a desire in some quarters to integrate more directive methods into person-centred therapy or to establish detailed and clearly defined contractual agreements with clients. Process researchers, too, have been keen to isolate micro-processes which can lead to more predictable outcomes and thus satisfy the demands of funding bodies or insurance companies. Most controversial, perhaps, is the position of the experiential therapists who claim to be a legitimate branch of the person-centred 'family' while placing emphasis on the client's ability to explore and integrate 'edge-of-awareness' experience through working with the bodily 'felt sense' indicator of such hidden material. The practice of 'focusing', originated and vigorously promoted by Eugene Gendlin, is employed by the experiential therapists as the primary method of accessing 'edge-of-awareness' experience and there can be little doubt about its effectiveness. What is more, focusing, because it is a well defined methodology and because it is undoubtedly effective for many clients in helping them to become more self-aware, is congenial to the *Zeitgeist* which gives high marks to articulated methods and predicable outcomes. The experientialists, for their part, can claim pragmatic brownie points while pointing to a practice which has about it many of the marks of a sophisticated secular meditation discipline. The critical issue, however, is whether the move into focusing can be a flight for the therapist from the challenge of entering into the kind of relational depth where greater spiritual truth can be encountered. Could it be that in facilitating greater self-awareness the experiential therapists are depriving their clients of the ultimate I–Thou encounter where the liberating mystery of being is experienced? Could it be that the client ends up in touch with his or her body, attuned to the inner flow of experience, emotionally literate and yet still alone and existentially bereft of meaning?

Differences and conflicts within the person-centred camp pale into comparative insignificance, when the notion of therapy as a spiritual process is placed in the context of the evolving world of counselling and psychotherapy in Britain, continental Europe and the United States of America. A culture which is permeated by the all-pervasive demands and allurements of materialistic consumerism is little interested in spiritual enlightenment. The increasing drivenness of many people, and the ravages of competitiveness and technological innovation, mean that quick 'cures' and a rapid return to functional efficiency are frequently demanded by clients who have neither the time nor the inclination to seek below the surface for the cause of their ills. In such a climate, therapeutic approaches which promise quick behavioural change, the immediate control of stress or the illumination of irrational thought patterns are highly acclaimed. Busy people with a constant eye on money and job security want rapid solutions and there is no lack of therapists and therapeutic orientations to respond to such needs. Perhaps a culture inevitably gets the kind of therapists which it deserves. And, after all, therapists, too, need to make their money and to render themselves employable by a Health Service or an Employee Assistance Programme, interested only in evidence-based therapy and quick returns for their investment.

This is not to say that I wish to dispute the potential efficaciousness of, for example, brief solution-focused therapy or the valuable contributions made to the relief of human suffering by cognitive behavioural therapy or, for that matter, by the astonishingly sophisticated forms of medication which are now available for the treatment of mental distress. I have no doubt whatever that there are countless individuals who have every reason to be profoundly grateful for the benefits that they have derived from such approaches (although there are also those who have been little helped). What I am suggesting, however, is that person-centred therapy with its central belief in the resourcefulness of the human being and its faith in the transformative power of relationship gives access to an altogether different domain. Person-centred therapy implicitly asserts that human beings are capable of the 'good life'; it is based on a 'positive psychology' which has as its starting point a vision of human beings as they have it within them to become. Such a becoming is prompted and enhanced by the power of relationship to engender a love of self, of the other and of the wider community so that the normal frontiers of experience can be transcended. It was the repeated confirmation of the sustainability of such a vision that Carl Rogers found in his later years not only in one-to-one relationships but also in small and large groups. His hope for a better world and his dedication to the mission of world peace were inspired by the experiential knowledge of men and women fully alive. Psychologists outside the humanistic tradition have recently pleaded for a resurgence of romanticism in psychotherapy, and Rogers can be seen as the precursor of such a development (Van Kalmthout 2000). While acknowledging the spirit of adventurous optimism conveyed by the nostalgic label of romanticism as a fitting description of one aspect of Rogers' personality, I myself would prefer to see him as a prophetic realist. The fact that our materialistic culture with its self-inflicted neuroses is beginning to tremble at its foundations and that more and more people are opting out before they succumb to its lethal seduction is, I would suggest, a possible sign of a very different order. The yearning for meaning and for a world where there is time to wait, to reflect and to relate will not be satisfied by the endeavours of counsellors and psychotherapists who collude with the desire for instant cures and the cost-effective application of magical techniques. Rogers may yet prove to be a prophetic realist who glimpsed the emptiness beyond the frenetic activity of 'new capitalist' men and women. By refusing to deny the mysterious energy released by the preparedness of persons to enter into relational depth with all their vulnerability and uncertainty, he opened up the possibility of new meaning and offered access to a mystical and spiritual world, which, until recently, psychology has derided and priests have often ceased to proclaim with conviction. This book is in many ways a celebration of Carl Rogers, the prophetic realist, and an elaboration of his tentative attempts to explore and describe the terrain which, almost despite himself, he found himself inhabiting. Perhaps – to use the concept of configurations of the Self – Rogers was not only a prophetic realist but also a reluctant mystic. It is scarcely surprising, then, that his legacy evokes such controversy.

CHAPTER 2

The human person: hope or despair?

One of the criticisms repeatedly made of Carl Rogers and his work is that he held to a naïvely optimistic view of human nature (cf. Thorne 1992). He is accused of failing to acknowledge the reality of evil and of paying scant attention to the 'shadow side' of human personality. An unpublished paper from the 1960s which eventually appeared in the Journal of Humanistic Psychology in 1995 attempted to forestall such criticisms:

> I do not have a Pollyanna view of human nature. I am quite aware that out of defensiveness and inner fear individuals can and do behave in ways which are horribly destructive, immature, regressive, anti-social, hurtful. Yet, one of the most refreshing and invigorating parts of my experience is to work with such individuals and to discover the strongly positive directional tendencies which exist in them, as in all of us, at the deepest levels.
>
> (Rogers 1995: 21)

This is an uncompromising statement for it extrapolates from Rogers' therapeutic experiences and points to a universal truth. The words 'as in all of us' leave no doubt that he believed that all human beings 'at the deepest levels' are motivated to move forward in ways which are positive, constructive and socially creative. At the same time, however, he cited 'defensiveness and inner fear' as potent causes for behaviour which can be anything but positive and life-enhancing. The statement in effect begs questions which demand answers. What, we might legitimately ask, is meant by the 'deepest levels' and what leads to the 'defensiveness and inner fear' which can so twist and pervert the innate tendency towards creative and constructive living?

Rogers' concept of the actualizing tendency is a metaphor of great richness. By it he postulated a sole motivating force which, if fully accessed, drives a person towards the accomplishment of his or her unique version of full humanness. It is the perfect metaphor for inspiring a life whose 'sole purpose is to grow'. Rogers later coined the term 'the formative tendency' to express the same notion of motivating energy as applied to the whole created order. The

9

metaphors are brilliantly appropriate in the context of an evolutionary model of both the human being and the universe. The parapsychologist, Rhea White, expresses another aspect of the same model when she writes: 'I think that the most viable aspect of humans is that both as a species and as individuals, no matter when, where or how long we live, we are unfinished creatures. Moreover, that is not our curse but our glory' (White 1997: 84).

Rich as the metaphors of the actualizing and formative tendencies are, they do not capture the essential interconnectedness either of human beings or of the natural world. It is clear from his painstaking exploration of the therapeutic relationship that Rogers did, in fact, see the human being as, by definition, relational, but this is not adequately addressed by the apparently non-relational metaphor of the actualizing tendency. Indeed, so serious a deficiency is this that it has led to the not infrequent accusation that person-centred therapy can bring about the cultivation of selfish monsters who are concerned solely with what *they* think, feel, desire or need with little or no regard for the consequences or for other people. In recent times, my colleague, Dave Mearns, and I have attempted to rescue the actualizing tendency from its purely organismic and non-relational interpretation by introducing the idea of 'social mediation' (Mearns and Thorne 2000). We are suggesting by this concept that the actualizing tendency can only be fully accessed and thereby be fully trustworthy when its motivating energy is tempered by the conscious reflection of the individual on the implications for his or her social relationships and the life of the wider community. Such a socially mediated actualizing tendency does justice, we believe, both to the organismically unique being of the biologically separate individual and to the intra- and interpersonal life of the essentially relational person who has the capacity as a psychological being for ever-increasing consciousness. This elaborated view of the actualizing tendency does not undermine Rogers' conviction that it is the sole motivating force for growth but, at the same time, it firmly acknowledges that self-consciousness and relational interdependence are essential characteristics of being human and are therefore not by definition in opposition to the actualizing tendency but need to be reflectively integrated into its promptings if the latter are to prove valid and trustworthy. In practice, this can lead to divergent behaviour among any group of persons because of their unique life stories. Where one person, for example, may need to reject the oppressive and stifling control of parental pressures in order to move closer to his or her unique fulfilment, another may need to hear the loving and authentic concern of parent or friend if he or she is not to behave self-destructively. What is more, the actualizing tendency, thus mediated, may whisper different messages at different times in a person's life. The young person, for example, may feel the desire to follow a course of action or a particular lifestyle but knows that he or she could not endure the anxiety or the condemnation which would ensue. With the passage of the years, however, what was impossible becomes a challenge which can be accepted willingly and courageously. It may be that it is possible through a re-working of such key concepts as the actualizing tendency to defend Rogers against some of the more virulent attacks on his so-called naïveté. His own response, however, was always to cite the evidence of his therapeutic experi-ence and it is to this that we now turn.

Rogers had great faith in the validity of his own experience and believed that, in the last analysis, there could be for him no superior guide to the living of a human life. This is a dangerous statement once it moves from a personal-ized response to take on the status of a universal dictum because it then fails to take account of the experiencer. Could it really be a tenable stance, for example, to credit the experience of a profoundly depressed person as being his or her best guide to living, let alone the experience of someone enduring paranoid delusions? Surely it is because, tragically, a paranoid person accepts his or her skewed perception as the guide to living that ghastly crimes are sometimes perpetrated. In the defence of his basically optimistic view of human nature Rogers nonetheless cites his experience as a therapist and as a group facilitator on repeated occasions. He maintains that among the persons with whom he has worked there have been those who were violent, delin-quent and self-destructive but that in all cases, once a therapeutic ambience has been established, these same persons have given evidence of positive and creative directional tendencies. I find this testimony persuasive not least because my own experience is strongly confirmatory of it. More than 30 years of therapeutic practice have shown me that if I can consistently offer the core conditions to another person, no matter how deep their wounded-ness and how powerful their self-destructive urges, there is every chance that, gradually, positive movement will occur and they will begin to embrace the hope that comes with self-acceptance. I am aware, however, that almost all my clients have *chosen* to come to me and that where this has not been the case – with some notable exceptions – it has not usually proved possible to stay in relationship long enough for the transformative process to get under way. For Rogers also it would be true to say that the vast majority of his clients and group members were 'self-referred' and that he writes little about those for whom this was not the case. The vast research project on institu-tionalized 'schizophrenic' patients which was carried out during Rogers' Wisconsin years was inconclusive in its findings about the effectiveness of person-centred therapy, although it should be remembered that Rogers himself was not personally involved as the therapist for most of these 'invol-untary' patients. What is more, doubt has been cast on the competence and even the therapeutic orientation of some of those practitioners who were participants in the project.

In summary, a case can perhaps be made for stating that the experience of Carl Rogers, Brian Thorne and doubtless of other person-centred therapists with self-referred clients points overwhelmingly to the conclusion that human beings have an innate tendency to develop in positive ways. The demonstrable fact that this does not occur for countless individuals who do not have the privilege of undergoing person-centred therapy with experienced practitioners can simply be attributed to their 'defensiveness and inner fear' which prevents them accessing their 'deepest levels'. It would be logical to conclude from such an assessment that the world would be a better place and human nature would have a far better chance of revealing its true glory if there were more person-centred therapists around who recognized the gravity of their existential responsibilities and had the competence to shoulder them. It is tempting to dismiss such an analysis as both hopelessly idealistic and ludicrously arrogant, but I wish to resist the temptation and to run the risk of being considered an inflated fool by pondering the matter further. What, after all, is being proffered as a diagnosis and as a remedy for the advancement of the human condition?

The diagnosis is decidedly dire. We are for the most part, it is suggested, frightened and defended creatures who have little sense of our own worth. We have arrived at this position principally because of the way others have treated us and because of the kind of society we have created. We spend most of our time in fear of judgement and condemnation and trying to win a modicum of approval to shore up our precarious self-esteem. We can even reach the point where we give up altogether and lapse into depression or decide literally or metaphorically to destroy ourselves and the rest of the world with us. Even those who have been dealt a better hand – such as those whom Maslow described towards the end of his life – can often be overwhelmed by the destructiveness or pointlessness of the world around them and lapse into indifference or impotent despair.

The remedy for this state of affairs lies in two core beliefs and in the way of being which springs from them. The first belief is that every human being is of infinite worth with a built-in actualizing tendency which if accessed and trusted can lead to the flowering of an uniquely fashioned humanness. The second belief is that we have a capacity to relate to ourselves and to others in such a way that our unique differences can be celebrated and that our corporate life can be enhanced. We can rejoice at one and the same time both in our individual uniqueness and in our corporate identity. From these two central beliefs there springs a way of being which is exemplified in the behaviour of the person-centred therapist and which also offers a blueprint for human relating and human community building in general. It was the passionate realization on Carl Rogers' part that what he had experienced and discovered in the therapy room had profound implications for life in general, which led him in the final part of his life to devote such energy to the creation of temporary communities and to the search for world peace.

I know that when I am being true to what I believe about human beings through my work as a therapist rather than simply mouthing platitudes in a conference hall, I am striving to live up to a demanding faith and practice:

> I believe that I am of infinite worth and all others with me.
>
> I believe that I need not be afraid of my inner world and must strive fearlessly to be in touch with it even if this is painful or confusing.
>
> I believe that it is my task to remain open to experience both inner and outer.
>
> I believe that the other deserves my understanding and not my judgement.
>
> I believe that to understand the other's world and to communicate that understanding is an essential part of being human.
>
> I believe that contractual living reduces human beings to commodities and that unfettered materialism destroys personhood.
>
> I believe that unconditional acceptance, both offered and received, dispels fear and opens up the path to authentic living.

The enormity of this expressed faith and with it my shaky conviction of its truth and power, despite its seemingly utopian aspirations, brings back to me with startling clarity the memory of a community where such a faith was lived out and where seeming miracles were almost a matter of routine. As I reflect today, I realize that my invincible hope in the potential greatness of human nature owes more than a little to my privileged experience of Finchden Manor (Burn 1956).

Finchden Manor was a therapeutic community for adolescent boys (although some girls were admitted towards the end of its existence) which was founded in the 1930s by a remarkable Cambridge historian turned therapist called George Lyward. It was housed in a rambling manor house at Tenterden in Kent and continued in existence until a year or so after Lyward's death in 1973. Lyward himself did not refer to his life's work as the creation of a therapeutic community. He spoke, rather, of providing a place of hospitality for those who had suffered severe psychological injury during their short lives and needed a respite (a favourite word) during which to draw breath and to have a second chance of growing up. Very few of the young residents at Finchden had chosen to be there in any normal sense of the word although, as far as I am aware, none were there under coercion or compulsory order. For many, however, Finchden Manor was their last hope. They had often experienced the whole gamut of expulsion from school, child guidance clinics and social and psychiatric services, and it was not uncommon to discover a history of delinquency (sometimes violent) which had landed them finally in the juvenile courts. It would be an altogether legitimate view to regard them as somewhat persuasive evidence of the essential darkness of human nature. Remarkably, however, almost all of them found healing and self-respect and not a few went on to become some of the most creative and distinguished members of their generation. Finchden Manor generated a transformational energy which substantiated Rogers' faith in the actualizing tendency in some of the most dramatic ways imaginable. To see the gradual metamorphosis of a bitter, self-hating and gratuitously delinquent teenager into a dynamic, intellectually and emotionally sophisticated, high-achieving young man was to witness an amazing journey from despair to hope, from self-vilification to mature self-affirmation.

Until I introduced him to the ideas of Carl Rogers, I am not sure that George Lyward had even heard of him. He certainly had little time for most psychological theorists and his opinion of conventional psychiatry was fairly unprintable. For me, however, it was possible to see the secret at the heart of Finchden Manor in terms of Lyward's ability to live out the theory and practice of person-centred therapy in a breathtakingly rigorous fashion. He used none of the jargon but his own language spoke of the same truths. He saw the boys who came to Finchden as the victims of what he called 'contractual living'. By this he meant that they could only win approval by fulfilling contracts established by others. He spoke of the 'I will love you if . . .' syndrome which did not have to be articulated to have a pervasively undermining influence in a young person's life. There was, in short, a total absence of unconditionality in their experiencing. Lyward also spoke frequently of the 'tyranny of fairness' by which he meant that parents, teachers and others were often so concerned to appear even-handed and without favourites that they failed entirely to honour the young person's unique identity and to devote any time whatever to understanding their inner world. As a result, there was no experience of authentic validation or of empathic understanding. Above all, Lyward saw that his young charges had grown up in a world populated by adults who for the most part sent out confusing signals which left their children bewildered and unable to gauge how to behave in order to win approval. It was a world permeated by hypocrisy, inconsistency and emotional blackmail parading as love. No wonder that in such an unpredictable emotional environment a young person would break down or resort to delinquency as a desperate attempt to draw attention to his inner fear and desolation. Alarmingly, the parents in such cases would often have little or no awareness of their own behaviour and its devastating consequences and would speak rather of only wanting what was best for the child or of having given him 'everything he asked for'. In the jargon of person-centred therapy, the parents were out of touch with their own flow of experience and were consequently in a state of incongruence and unable to offer to others a dependable authenticity.

When an adolescent arrived at Finchden Manor he discovered to his amazement an environment without demands. There was no insistence on

achieving goals or meeting standards and no special privileges to be gained
by currying favour. All that was required, it seemed, was a willingness to be
honest and not to pretend. Initially terrifying because so utterly unfamiliar,
this environment gradually induced a level of relaxation and a reduction in
the fear of judgement which made it possible for the young person to stop
and to listen to himself. He then discovered that Lyward and his staff and,
perhaps more importantly, his fellow 'guests' were actually interested in
what he discovered. Finchden was a place where it was possible not to get up
until mid-day (although you could not expect breakfast then), to wander in
the grounds without being questioned, to persuade others to play cricket if
you wanted to and to find yourself quite unexpectedly in deep conversation
with someone about the pain of having an unhappy, nagging mother. After a
year or two you might even discover that you had become intellectually
insatiable and needed to study for an A Level. Of course, Lyward was the ever-
present (even when he was absent) genius of the place. His ability to offer
unconditional validation, to enter into the inner worlds of those who invited
him there and to be at all times authentic in his dealings with others – even to
the expression of towering anger on occasion – all this was infectious, often
at an unconscious level, and led to the creation of a community where loving
and being loved were experienced as part of the same activity. What is more,
it quickly became apparent, even to the most lonely and alienated teenager,
that he had the capacity and the need to love as well as the need to be loved
and that he was acceptable in both roles.

The work of George Lyward during more than 40 years, and the remarkable success of Finchden Manor in rescuing damaged adolescents from a life
of bitter self-denigration, serve to reinforce yet further the belief in the essential capacity of human beings to live creatively and hopefully once they are
given the opportunity to access the core of their own natures. Lyward's
astonishing accomplishment makes it difficult to accept that there are those
who are fundamentally motivated by the desire to destroy themselves and
others even if much of their behaviour had previously seemed to point
inexorably in that direction. Just as Carl Rogers' clients and my own provide
overwhelming evidence of human resilience and creativity, even more so do
Lyward's damaged, angry and self-punitive 'guests' demonstrate the capacity
of the human spirit to be re-born to new hope and new possibilities. The
determining factor, it seems, is the quality of relationship they are offered and
the chance to discover their own innate ability to love. Perhaps that is the
reason why Finchden Manor always had a resident population of dogs, cats
and other animals. It is often easier initially to love an animal passionately and
to find that love accepted and reciprocated than it is to take the risk of being
rejected by a human being when experience has confirmed that so-called
love is usually abusive, manipulative or demanding.

Am I returning, by the circuitous route of Finchden Manor, to the conviction that human nature is essentially positive as long as it is given the chance to flourish? If I am to be faithful to my own experience I am left, in the end, with no alternative but to embrace this conviction. What, then, am I to make of those affirmed and talented persons of whom Abraham Maslow despaired, let alone of such a phenomenon as the much vilified Adolf Hitler who is predictably portrayed as the ultimate proof of human evil? It would be possible simply to dismiss Hitler and other notable murderous tyrants as exceptions to the general rule, and Maslow's loved but apathetic persons as the victims not of their own natures but of the overwhelming negativity by which they were surrounded. My experience of Finchden Manor and some of my most demanding encounters with clients lead me to further reflections which received support from my recent reading of a massive study edited by Ronald Rosenbaum on the origins of Hitler's evil (Rosenbaum 1998).

The outcome of Rosenbaum's detailed and exhaustive undertaking is essentially inconclusive. Various hypotheses are advanced and, although some are more persuasive than others, none are adequate to explain the enormity of Hitler's malevolence and deliberately murderous undertakings. The mystery is almost certainly insoluble and will remain as a sinister conundrum for historians and psychologists for all time. I was struck, however, by one significant fact. It would seem that, although Hitler was clearly admired and all but worshipped by thousands – many known to him personally – there is no recorded instance of his own loving being welcomed and deeply desired. On the contrary, there is some evidence that a particularly unpleasant sexual perversion contaminated his intimate relationships and led to the suicide or murder of the one woman whom he genuinely loved. Hitler never escaped from loneliness: at the height of his power he remained an outsider.

The healing power of Finchden Manor resided in its capacity to counteract precisely such alienation. Lyward once remarked that the first time he stood in front of a class of children he became aware that he and they were all essentially interlinked – they were members one of another. It followed from this realization that nobody was superfluous and that everyone was both a transmitter and a receiver of validating energy. Finchden Manor somehow exemplified this fundamental understanding of the human condition. As a result, each member of the community gradually came to realize that his loving was both needed and valued and that without it the community was impoverished. For a Finchden boy to be accepted was wonderful but to discover that his acceptance and valuing of others was vital to the wellbeing of the community meant the end of alienation.

As I think of some of the most challenging clients I have encountered during my lengthy career as a therapist, I know that most of them have required that I accept their love. Not to do so would be to send the message that their loving – however imperfect or possessive or demanding – was essentially destructive, and such a judgement, however subtly disguised, would be to condemn them to continuing alienation and to a sense of their unworthiness to be a part of the human family. To put the matter concisely and starkly, I conclude from the loving but often difficult responses of my clients, from the remarkable interdependence of the Finchden community and from the apparent perversity and unacceptability of Hitler's loving that human nature is indeed positive and trustworthy if it is given the chance to flourish. Not to be able to love, however, or to have one's love rejected or condemned is to ensure that such flourishing has no chance. On the contrary, confirmed in the role of the alienated outsider, the rejected lover – no matter how understandable or predictable the rejection – is in danger of becoming the very opposite of what he or she has the potential to be. Could it be that hope for the evolution of the human race depends upon an ability to catch the movements of love within ourselves and within others and to ensure that they are never squandered no matter how difficult it may be to give them expression or to receive them without fear?

CHAPTER 3

The therapeutic relationship: professional contract or existential encounter

One of the things that makes me angry these days, if I allow myself to reflect on it long enough, is the absurd salaries earned by some lawyers and accountants. When I read that the current Prime Minister's wife can command £200 000 a year and that accountants who land up as Managing Directors can treble that figure, I sense within myself the kind of disproportionate rage that can fire revolutions and lead to the barricades. It is not that I am particularly incensed by the individuals themselves: it is rather than I am overwhelmed by an impotent despair at the culture which has arrived at so perverse a scale of values. What counts, it would seem, is the ability to manipulate the money market and the rapier-like cleverness which thrives in the world of the contractual jungle.

Perhaps it is the connection between lawyers and contracts which sends shudders down my spine when I embark on some of my therapeutic relationships nowadays, for contracts have come to have a prominent place in the ethical codes of practice for therapists. In principle, of course, there is nothing sinister in such a development. It is clearly right that clients should know what to expect of their therapists, that they should have an understanding, as far as is possible, of the likely processes they will undergo and agree to the administrative and, where appropriate, the financial arrangements involved. The difficulty arises when the requirement to establish a contract at the outset runs counter to the manifest demands of the existential encounter. If, as the therapist, I am preoccupied with the requirement to establish a contract with my client in order not to be arraigned subsequently for unethical behaviour, it is more than likely that I shall fail to meet my client in his or her distress and by observing the letter of the ethical code I shall convey the message that I cannot or will not enter the relationship until I am contractually engaged. I am reminded of the story of the American physician who would not respond to the needs of a person struck down by a potentially lethal heart attack on the airport tarmac because the unfortunate victim could not produce evidence of his medical insurance. Contracts, often designed to ensure justice and protect the vulnerable from abuse, can lead to a withering of the heart which sounds the likely death knell to the encounter which can heal. If, in the face of a weeping and desperate fellow human being, I am preoccupied with the necessity of explaining my therapeutic orientation and establishing a mutually acceptable contract for our work together, it may well be that I shall fail to be truly present and that he or she will not experience my preparedness to risk myself in a relationship which cannot be controlled or prescribed in advance. Such a failure may have serious repercussions. Invitations to deep encounter, whether made deliberately or unwittingly, are seldom repeated if they are once rejected or their acceptance hedged around with reservations and conditions. A movement of love can be stifled by the therapist's fear of being accused of contractual negligence or by the client's dismay at meeting a fearful hesitancy rather than wholehearted acceptance.

My discomfort at the prominence given to establishing detailed contracts is reinforced by a similar emphasis in some ethical codes on the maintenance of clearly defined boundaries. Again, it is obviously right that clients should be protected from invasive therapists and from those who abuse their power by changing the parameters of the therapeutic relationship without warning and without regard for the client's needs and wishes or with scant respect for his or her vulnerability. Insistence on boundaries is rightly emphasized so that the client can feel safe from the unwelcome attentions of abusive therapists or of those whose self-deception or self-inflation is so great that they exercise their personal power without awareness of their responsibility. On the other hand, the very notion of a boundary – especially a rigidly prescribed one – speaks of a 'so far but no further' mentality. It suggests an unwillingness to venture into unknown terrain, the unexplored 'no-man's land' where almost inevitably those who have suffered most need to venture if they are to face the depths of their pain and their terror. The therapist who is prepared to be a companion in such terrain must sometimes move across a boundary courageously or risk leaving the client stranded in a place of fear to which is then added the desolation of abandonment. A boundary which says or implies that as a therapist I must, for example, never extend a session beyond its normal time limit, that I must never touch my client, that I must never give my home telephone number, that I must never accept gifts, that I must never acknowledge my own vulnerability – all such prohibitions (sometimes altogether reasonable and conducive to the client's development) can wreak havoc if they prevent a welcoming response to a person's first tentative expression of their yearning for love or of their profound desire to offer love. I become increasingly convinced that the insistence on maintaining boundaries often springs from a fear of so-called over-involvement and is – perhaps unconsciously – aimed at protecting therapists from the messy relationships with clients which often result when the journey into no-man's land begins in earnest. The result, I believe, has been the emergence of a therapeutic norm of *under-involvement*, whether this be encouraged by the imposition of ethical codes which have a constant eye on the hostile manoeuvres of an increasingly litigious population or by a finance-driven move towards short-term therapy or solution-focused approaches which, it is claimed, are congenial to clients who want to get on with their lives and have little patience with unprofitable introspection. Such under-involvement is then defended and rationalized as ethically responsible and in keeping with therapeutic advances appropriate to an age which is always in a hurry and where apparent cost-effectiveness often seems of far greater importance than therapeutic efficacy.

Perhaps the greatest rationalization of all, however, is the retreat into a pseudo-professionalism. This particular stance presents the detailed contract, the rigid observance of boundaries and the commitment to empirically validated (whatever that means) therapies as the necessary hallmark of a true professionalism appropriate to twenty-first-century men and women. By implication, those approaches which view human beings as anything but predictable and remain open to the evolution of humankind through the journey into relationship and the mystical apprehension of a transcendental reality are in danger of losing their professional credibility and finding themselves pilloried as little more than endearing mythologies of yesteryear. In such a climate it is easy to forget that person-centred therapy remains one of the most researched therapeutic approaches in the world and that the powerful effectiveness of the core conditions has never been convincingly disproved. I am reminded of a conversation I once had over 30 years ago with George Lyward as he returned to his study after saying goodbye to a group of visiting psychiatrists. 'You know,' he said, 'most of these professionals who visit us are appalled by what they see. They cannot understand the lack of rules, the apparent chaos, the absence of structures. They simply don't understand that it is precisely rules, structures, the letter of the law that have driven our young people to despair in the first place. What good would it do if we simply repeated the same barbarism? And then they can't understand why we're successful. I think they believe I'm some sort of magician, not just a human being doing his best to be human.' Years later I remember Carl Rogers observing that, as therapists, who we are is good enough as long as we can just be it openly. Everything, it seems, depends upon our commit-ment to becoming the people we have it within us to be. For the person-centred therapist this makes for a peculiarly paradoxical kind of professionalism. So often, professionalism results from the possession of specialized knowledge and skills which others need for the conduct of their lives. For the person-centred therapist, however, the knowledge and the skills reside in the courage and the capacity to become more fully human so that others in turn may discover confidence in their own human resourcefulness. A strange profession indeed which requires of its practitioners that they simply become more fully themselves.

Put like that, the professionalism of the person-centred therapist can sound breathtakingly selfish. The corrective comes from two sources. In the first place if, as I believe, human nature is essentially relational, it follows that the more I can become myself, the more I shall both need and want the other for my completion. Secondly – and of supreme importance – the decision to be a therapist implies a willing commitment to the service of others. If such a commitment is not present it is difficult to see the work of the therapist as little more than a means of earning money or of acquiring status. In recent times the fear of being labelled a 'do-gooder' has made many people in the helping professions reluctant to acknowledge their altruistic motivation and person-centred therapists have not been exempt from this reluctance. This is not to deny that the desire to be loved is commonly a strong motivating force in the decision to become a therapist but this in no way diminishes the accompanying altruistic dedication to finding meaning in the service of others. Person-centred therapists, then, are required by their profession to become more fully themselves but they choose to do so because, by so doing, they can be more effective companions to those who seek their help. The self-love which makes it possible to continue growing, despite the fear and pain which this often entails, at the same time inspires the self-forgetfulness which the service of others frequently demands. Personal growth and professional effectiveness are undoubtedly linked, and there is no escaping the fact that both the personal and the professional stature of the person-centred therapist are on trial the moment the client enters the room or, in some cases, the moment they pick up the phone. It is the existential encounter which reveals whether the therapist is enough of a person to be able to assume the professional responsibility which the therapeutic relationship requires. No amount of contracting can compensate for the therapist's lack of personal resourcefulness and no amount of fine talk about methods and goals can conceal the inability of the therapist to meet the client as person to person.

One of the most hopeful signs that perhaps the tide is beginning to turn and that ethical codes of rigid complexity are coming to be seen as the enemy of good and creative practice is the announcement of the British Association for Counselling and Psychotherapy that, as from April 1 2002, a new Statement of Fundamental Ethics for Counselling and Psychotherapy is to become operative. This new document, although subject to amendment in the light of a current consultation process, comes like a blast of fresh air into the increasingly arid and potentially punitive ethical scene. Its emphasis on values, principles and the personal qualities of the therapist promises a framework for practice which is altogether more respectful of the practitioner's integrity, courage and commitment. It comes at a time when the statutory regulation of the psychological therapies seems increasingly likely and imminent. Time alone will tell whether it will carry the day when the transition to this regulated era actually takes place. For person-centred therapists, however, there is new hope where previously the outlook had seemed depressingly bleak. This new 'statement' is bold enough to acknowledge that 'No statement of ethics can totally alleviate the difficulty of making professional judgements in circumstances that may be constantly changing and full of uncertainties.' Furthermore, the Association commits its members 'to engaging with the challenge of striving to be ethical, even when doing so involves making difficult decisions or acting courageously' (BACP 2001: 5). Such language suggests a mindset which stands in glorious contrast to the detailed and legalistic rulebookese which tended to characterize the Association's codes and procedures of the past.

More needs to be said about the therapist's self-love, which I am suggesting is a prerequisite for offering a relationship within which, in the course of an efficient interaction with a professional who is contractually protected, the client can hope to experience a transformative encounter with a person whose professional commitment is precisely to be fully a person. The scope for the misunderstanding of these concepts is immense. For many people, the notion of self-love is immediately confused with selfishness and self-inflation. Such fundamental misunderstanding can lead to the perception of the self-loving person as someone who is arrogant, concerned only with his or her own self-interest and whose sense of self-importance precludes any meaningful relationship with others. Self-love, correctly understood, leads to the very opposite of these characteristics. The self-loving person experiences so profound a level of self-acceptance that he or she is no longer self-preoccupied. Such a person does not have to be constantly concerned about the judgement of others or about the creation of an impressive image or façade. To be self-loving is to be released into a freedom from anxiety about rejection, abandonment or condemnation. This is not to say that such a person is spared from pain if he or she is rejected or condemned but it does mean that the pain or guilt will not lead to self-negation or despair. The self-loving person is no longer a problem to himself or herself and is therefore free to enter into relationship without fear.

How, it might be asked, is such self-love attained? This is a question of the most profound importance not least because it is evident that self-love, as I have defined and illustrated it above, is not greatly in evidence in our culture. On the contrary, there can scarcely be a more image-conscious era than our own, where a person's self-esteem seems to depend increasingly on material possessions, achievements or even, if we are to believe current research on youngsters, on physical appearance. Self-love may be nourished or enhanced by such factors but it is essentially independent of them. It comes from an unshakeable belief in the unique value of the human person and the essential wonder of the human race, together with the logical realization that one is not oneself exempt from such a belief but a living embodiment of it. To live out such a belief demands not arrogance but the humility to accept the truth about the essential core of one's own being. Sadly, however, it is precisely this core which few seem to glimpse let alone come to define as the key to their humanity.

The truly self-loving therapist has not only glimpsed the core of his or her own being but has discovered how to hold it in consciousness and to stay in contact with it. Such 'in touchness' becomes a professional imperative for the person-centred therapist if he or she is not to become fraudulent in his or her dealings with clients. To offer unconditional acceptance and deep under-standing to another while withholding it from oneself is to risk an under-mining contradiction at the centre of the therapeutic endeavour. For the person-centred therapist there is no alternative but to ensure that there are others who can hold up to him or her a mirror fashioned by respect, tender-ness and understanding so that a loving attitude to self is maintained from which can flow a spontaneous response of validation and affirmation to those who seek help because they have lost – or perhaps have never found – any sense of their own loveliness.

Those who work with the severely disturbed usually discover that such people have no sense of their own worth or that little in their past lives has encouraged them to think of themselves with love or respect. On the contrary, it would seem that acceptance and empathy have often been in grossly short supply in the experience of those who have succumbed to severe mental distress or disintegration (cf. Biermann-Ratjen 1998; Binder 1998). The human infant is wholly dependent on others to offer a mirror in which he or she can see reflected a true image. Those who offer the child no empathy and no acceptance, or who only do so intermittently, provide a distorting mirror or no mirror at all so that the child develops without the assurance of the essential validity of his or her own identity. On the contrary, there is more likely to be a sense of confusion or of shame because all that has been glimpsed is the image of a person who is apparently unworthy of love or even of the most fleeting attention. Such persons, coming as adults to a therapist, are in despair because they do not know who they are but suspect that they are utterly without value or even, in some cases, that they are evil.

Those whose self-concepts have become so far divorced from their intrinsic worth as human beings that they can think of themselves as evil throw a shocking but revealing shaft of light on the task of the therapist. It may be that those of us who practise as person-centred therapists have grown accustomed to being with those who have lost touch with their own worth and consider themselves to be 'hopeless cases' or 'life's failures'. We know something of the arduous journey from this position of self-denigration to a place where self-acceptance seems possible and the restoration or discovery of self-esteem becomes a reality. We know, too, the cost of such a journey in terms of our own constancy and unremitting commitment to empathic acceptance and authentic relationship. To be with a person who believes, however, that he or she has fallen into the grips of evil has about it an altogether different intensity.

Such a person may be terrified or defiant. Dave Mearns in 'Person-Centred Therapy Today' (Mearns and Thorne 2000) describes a client who willingly and deliberately claimed the title 'evil' because this enabled him to defend himself against the destructive forces by which he was surrounded. If he was evil then it made sense to put the dagger in first because, in that way, he would not be destroyed. To become the oppressor or destroyer is a foolproof way of avoiding annihilation. To be an evil person in this kind of context rationalizes and, in a curious way, justifies behaviour which would otherwise be totally without meaning. The defiance inherent in such a stance is fuelled by the desperate energy required for survival.

There are others, however, who, far from courting evil in order to defend themselves, find that they are powerless to resist overwhelming internal urges to destroy and to inflict harm. They are evil in their own eyes because they seem to have no control over these urges and fear that they will perpetrate monstrous crimes of violence and hatred. Some may succumb to mental illness and feel compelled to commit murder and other atrocities in order to obey voices and powers which they experience as possessing absolute authority. Such tragic cases often reach the front pages of our newspapers and trigger venomous hatred and fear of all those who are mentally ill, irrespective of their condition. To put it concisely and bluntly, the person-centred therapist in the presence of such persons becomes the representative of the forces of light against the powers of darkness.

Perhaps it matters how such powers are conceptualized by the therapist. If I believe that nobody is evil and that so called evil thoughts and behaviour are the outcome of life's experiences and sufferings whether deliberately or defiantly owned or impotently and fearfully experienced, this will clearly influence both my feelings and my behaviour in response to such persons. If, again, I subscribe to certain understandings of mental illness, I shall be rightly concerned to enable some of my highly disturbed clients to find psychiatric help and medication which will restore the chemical balance in their bruised and battered brains. If I have a view of evil which encompasses cosmic forces in the invisible world about us and beyond the threshold of death, I may well wish to tap into resources traditionally associated with the prayers, rituals, sacraments and doctrines of the world's great religions. What, if I am honest, I shall not be able to do is trivialize my role or the immense implications of my client's condition. I am forced to take seriously the responsibility of being a representative of the forces of light in a world where the powers of darkness – however conceptualized – are often ferociously active and threaten life, sanity and the very fabric of society and of our planetary environment.

I do not believe that for the person-centred therapist the self-concept of being a representative of the forces of light is either incongruous or illogical. It may be a frightening idea and daunting in the extreme because the risks of self-inflation, self-deception or simply blatant inadequacy are clearly legion. If, however, I believe – as person-centred therapists claim to do – that human beings are infinitely resourceful and have immense capacities for self-understanding, creativity and empathic responsiveness, it is surely not unreasonable to expect person-centred therapists to be committed to the path that has as its destination what Rogers himself described in the most prosaic terminology imaginable as the fully functioning person. It is evident, however, that there is a marked reluctance on the part of many person-centred practitioners to claim what may seem to them to be such a grandiose and even arrogant aspiration. 'Don't expect me to be a saint' is often the cry of many a trainee but these days I am tempted (if that is the appropriate word!) to reply, 'Why not? Don't you want to be someone who is committed to living life to the full and to finding the courage to be a light in the world?' Nothing less, I have come to believe, is required by increasing numbers of our clients, and perhaps the time has come for us to acknowledge that to be fully professional as person-centred therapists leaves us with no option. We are required to be lights in the darkness whether we like it or not and we need to be clear that our relationships with our clients will sometimes take place in a world whose laws and rules may bear only a faint resemblance to the Codes of Ethics and Practice which we have pinned to our consulting room walls.

CHAPTER 4

The person-centred therapist as secular priest and prophet

Lionel Blue, the well-known Jewish rabbi, volunteered the information, in a recent talk to the Norfolk Theological Society, that many rabbis had become therapists and that perhaps this was the most useful work they could do in the future. I am also aware that almost every year the cohorts of trainees I have welcomed at the University of East Anglia have contained priests or ministers who, for the most part, had grown weary of or angry with their religious institutions. The ranks of the therapists, it would seem, are increasingly swollen by numbers of disenchanted clergy who are either seeking an alternative role altogether or hoping to find a way of giving new life to their pastoral ministries. At the risk of over-simplification, it would be possible to see some of these frustrated priests as persons who are attempting to equip themselves for work in a culture which seems increasingly sceptical about religion while being convinced – sometimes passionately – about the central importance of spirituality. They want to be able to respond to those who are often desperate to find meaning and a sense of interconnectedness in a world which is experienced as empty, fragmented, rudderless and programmed for destruction. What is more, such spiritual seekers do not necessarily expect clarity or powerful intellectual argument, let alone authoritative maps of the spiritual world. They yearn, rather, for sensitive accompaniment from someone who, like them, can no longer remain on the surface of life, as a hapless prisoner of the banalities of materialistic consumerism. They sense that the resources for living a life of depth and meaning lie within themselves and in the world around them. They have lost, however, the means of accessing the riches which they dimly sense but cannot embrace. The priest turned counsellor hopes that, in the new role, he or she will be a more effective companion for such people whose spiritual path lies veiled in the mists of doubt, uncertainty and, often, fear.

Carl Rogers withdrew from his training as a Christian minister because he could no longer endure the prospect of being the representative of an institution which required of him a professed commitment to a set of beliefs and dogmas and entrusted him with the task of preaching and proclaiming them. Indeed, it was the experience of having to get up in front of a congregation and preach which finally determined him to renounce the goal to which he had aspired for many years. Later he was to refer to the 'chains of dogma' which he believed had come to afflict the followers of Freud (Rogers 1959: 191), but as a young man it was the chains of institutional religion which he knew he had to shake off if he was to be free to be true to himself and, subsequently, to those who would seek his help. It would seem that for him as a man of his time and culture, and given his own family conditioning, the shaking off of his Christian beliefs and practice meant turning his back on the spiritual world altogether. It was to be many years later before he could once more allow himself to enter a depth of experiencing where, almost reluctantly, he found himself acknowledging phenomena for which only the language of the spiritual and the mystical seemed adequate. It is interesting to speculate, however, whether Rogers, in fact, abandoned his career as a minister of religion so that, without being conscious of it at the time, he might embrace an altogether more influential and powerful role as a spiritual leader of the future. Certainly many of those who now seek training as person-centred therapists are consciously pursuing a spiritual vocation, and that undoubtedly applies to many who are already priests or ministers whether or not they consciously intend to abandon those roles altogether. It is also by no means unknown for clergy who at the start of their therapeutic training have no intention of leaving the priesthood to discover that the more they relate in depth with clients, the more unattractive it becomes to return to a role where institutional trappings impede the development of the very kind of relationships which now give them such satisfaction and where – more significantly – they experience themselves as channels of spiritual energy in a way which was not possible when they were trapped in the institutional role. I have known a number of sincere and devout clergy who have given the best part of their lives to the Church but have reluctantly and painfully come to the realization that the institution which they have loved and served can no longer sustain them in their own spiritual journey or in the work which they feel called to do.

It would seem that the time is now past when, in Britain at any rate, most people could feel comfortable about approaching the clergy with their personal problems and concerns. The somewhat grandiose claims of the Church of England vicar or rector, for example, to be the pastor to all those living in the parish and not just simply to the worshipping congregation has little meaning for most of the potential recipients of such care. It is perhaps a mark of the gulf which now exists between the churches and the majority of the population that in urban areas most people will be unaware even of the location of their parish church and will have no idea of who the vicar is or what he does apart from taking a service or two on a Sunday. Those clergy who present themselves for training as therapists often speak of themselves – somewhat despairingly – as the officers of an antiquated club surviving off its historical fat and with an ageing membership more inclined to whinge than to exude the joy which comes from knowing the presence of God. It is true that there have sprung up in recent years a number of so-called house churches or spiritual communities – usually led by zealous laymen or women rather than by clergy – but these, while often providing initial security and affirmation for lonely and perhaps vulnerable people, can become at a later stage a source of oppression and manipulation prompted by the questionable motives of power-hungry leaders. Some of the more extreme examples of such emotional coercion have led to appalling outcomes which have rocked the world. It is often claimed that the mainstream churches, whatever their shortcomings, because of their various checks and balances are less likely to give rise to such explosive and profoundly destructive processes. While this may be broadly true, the recent spate of horrific cases of sexual abuse involving clergy must cast doubt on the ability of a church, however structured and regulated, to control its more wayward and damaging members. It is also not irrelevant that the cases of sexual abuse sometimes involve clergy whose own level of sexual and emotional maturity has been in their own view at best stunted and at worst impaired by their vocational training and the perceived requirements of their priestly role. It would seem that the public perception of the clergy as inadequately equipped to respond to emotional and relationship concerns has been tragically reinforced by this proliferation of scandals in recent times which, we are told, may not abate in the years ahead as more offences come to light, some dating back for decades.

With the Church's poor press, the ridicule to which some of its doctrines and moral stances are subjected and the blatantly inadequate and even criminally culpable behaviour of some of its clergy, it might be expected that there would be few people wishing to put themselves forward for ordination at this time. Interestingly, the picture is by no means so clear-cut. The Church of England presents a particularly intriguing pattern for it would seem that after many years of decline the numbers coming forward are on the increase. The admission of women to the priesthood is a strong contributory factor to this state of affairs, as is also the recruitment of many persons in their middle years to locally ordained ministry. The profile of candidates has changed radically and with it, perhaps, the likely role of the priest of the future. It is not altogether fanciful to suppose that we shall see the emergence – in the Church of England at least – of a priesthood much more skilled in human relationships and informed by the experience of family life (not least as mothers) and of a variety of work contexts. If this indeed occurs we could see the gradual reinstatement of the priest as a resource person for the whole community because he or she is perceived not as the representative of an institution and the embodiment of a belief system but as a human being skilled in emotional accompaniment and unafraid to point to a reality which values the quality of being above achievement and material possessions.

The forerunner of such a priesthood may well turn out to be the Reverend Peter Owen Jones, the rector of three rural parishes near Cambridge, who was daring and honest enough to present to the world his personal diary for the year 1998–99 in the form of an astonishing publication entitled *Small Boat, Big Sea* (2000). This diary contains within it the pointers towards a concept of priesthood which may serve as a beacon of light in a dark world because it is nourished by a spirituality which embraces the interconnectedness of persons and the created order, and sees the unconditionality of divine love as its source. Owen Jones reveals himself in his diaries to be – in person-centred terms – a remarkably congruent person. He is scrupulously attentive to his thoughts and feelings and stays fearlessly with them no matter how painful or perplexing they may be. There is no trace in this man of a retreat into role or dogma as a way of protecting himself from pain or of evading confrontation with challenging aspects of his own experience. Remarkably, however, such congruence does not lead to despair or to a cynical rejection of the Church with all its infuriating habits and less than perfect members. Instead, Owen Jones, without abandoning the structures, discovers a way of being a priest which carries conviction for him and makes sense of the context of the so-called postmodern world. What is startling, however, is the remarkable convergence with much that is familiar in person-centred philosophy and practice.

Perhaps more than the therapist, the priest can be in thrall to his or her role. The wearing of a dog-collar or the robes of priestly office proclaims the 'apartness' or professionalism of the priest even more than the therapist's certificate of accreditation and the ethical codes of practice pinned on the wall. And yet both priest and therapist are in the business of relating in depth and of accompanying others into the unknown where pain and joy are likely to be present in equal measure. Not to relate in depth and not to be prepared to enter the mysterious unknown is to make a mockery of both professions. What is the use of a therapist or of a priest who clings to safety and refuses to engage other than superficially or according to a manualized set of instructions? Owen Jones knows the dilemma well:

To be honest, individual personality simply gets in the way most of the time and you are left with these two people, the person you are and the person you have become. The tension between the two is fantastic; the role is so seductive but role-playing simply means I cannot handle it. My masculinity, my sexuality is surrendered; it becomes unimportant and is redefined in the whites of other people's eyes. We are not meant to desire, you see, we are not supposed to look down the line that leads into the dark along the skin formed when thighs are crossed, we are not meant to get angry . . . When the role takes over completely and the gap between the person and the priest becomes a gulf, then you are in real trouble. Some people end up as Jekyll and Hyde.

(Owen Jones 2000: 36–7)

As Owen Jones struggles to be honest with himself, the more he is forced to face what it is he truly believes about God:

Despite my genuinely dreadful behaviour I can only say that the God that I experience is one of infinite patience and love and it is always my own lack of courage to face up to that, to accept it for what it is that creates the tensions that lead to loneliness. This inner loneliness, which is ultimately a denial of soul, is the greatest disease of our age. It is the sub-plot for so much. It is the grace of God that ultimately saves us all.

(Owen Jones 2000: 222)

This commitment to searing honesty with himself allows Owen Jones to acknowledge that it is the refusal to accept the love of a God who is infinitely accepting and patient that leads to the desolation of the soul. It is not difficult to equate such a theological insight with the person-centred insistence on self-love as the prerequisite for the effective therapist. The experience of being unconditionally accepted and its deep internalization is as necessary for the therapist as it is for the priest; and Owen Jones acknowledges that for him to believe in a God who offers precisely such acceptance is difficult enough, but to have the courage to live out such a belief is infinitely more challenging.

If the tension between the personal and the professional and the struggle to be self-loving are experiences that the priest and the person-centred therapist have in common, so, too, is the response to the prevailing consumerist culture which places both priest and therapist on the margins of contemporary society even if they attempt to deny the reality of their exclusion. In his diary Owen Jones does not attempt to conceal that he is in almost permanent trouble with his bank manager:

By the standards of the Third World we are outrageously wealthy but we do not live in the third world and by the standards of this country we are not well off at all. Every week is a struggle and we are in deep debt. If it was just me I wouldn't be bothered by it, I really could be happy to eat dust. It's when other people are depending on you that it becomes critical. Being crap with money and mindlessly extravagant is probably at the root of it all – it makes our friend's chickens harder to swallow.

(Owen Jones 2000: 109)

The priest is by definition the enemy of rampant consumerism. He or she points to a truth which feeds the inner life and not to a clever strategy for ensuring a comfortable external life buttressed by possessions and material security:

> Our society does not recognize the inner life at all, the inner person, not until they need a hospital. Peace has become something that you can find in a hammock on the Caribbean, love has been defined by sex, truth by advertising. In the West we are physically fat but our inner selves are starving.
>
> (Owen Jones 2000: 177–78)

As the Church loses its position of prestige in society and faces the unpalatable fact that (to the majority of people) it is at best peripheral and at worst irrelevant, so its central message of love and being is revealed as utterly counter-cultural in the West. As the money runs out, priests are forced to recognize that the so-called 'bias to the poor' is not an interesting theological concept but the inevitable consequence of beliefs and values which see the accumulation of material possessions as the enemy of the spirit and the root of injustice in the world. Owen Jones, in a moment of Franciscan extremism, sees the radical challenge and is electrified by it:

> I believe now that truly to follow God, quite literally, means that some of us may want to give up what we have and take to the roads, sleep in what's left of the hedges, freeze in February, burn in July. It's not so ridiculous. I will do it one day.
>
> (Owen Jones 2000: 71)

For the person-centred therapist such mad idealism may seem far removed from the hurly burly of the therapeutic marketplace where different orientations compete for clients and vie with each other in their extravagant claims. And yet it would seem that person-centred therapy is not greatly favoured by those who hold the purse strings. It is somehow too vague and indeterminate for them in its goals and objectives and too idiosyncratic in its implementation. Its heavy emphasis on the creation of relationship and its trust in the client's ability to know what is best do not sit comfortably with the current obsessional need for rapid results and the accurate evaluation of outcome. Person-centred therapists watch with alarm as they see the approach which they practise marginalized, misunderstood and even denigrated by those who trumpet the efficacy of their particular brand of therapy and point to its cost-effectiveness. It is a tough world and both in Europe and the United States person-centred therapists and other humanistic practitioners often find themselves on the wrong side of new laws and regulations and, as a consequence, deprived of state funds and the benevolent co-operation of insurance companies. Those who have trained as person-centred therapists and have done so with enthusiasm and conviction are sometimes faced with stark choices: either they must re-train in methodologies for which they have little sympathy or they must face the possibility of going it alone and trusting that the clients who need them will still find their way to their door. It is certainly not an option that promises much financial security. Indeed, in many contexts it would seem that the person-centred therapist who chooses to remain faithful to his or her approach may well be courting a life of financial unpredictability at best and financial disaster at worst.

It is intriguing to say the least that as person-centred therapists in Britain fight hard – and with justification – to lay claim to a rightful place in the mainstream of therapeutic practice, to be part of the 'establishment' as it were, so priests like Peter Owen Jones recognize that it is the very fact of 'establishment' which makes the Church of England particularly repellent to many and so constraining for others:

> . . . there is a tension, a huge tension between this wild and intimate source of the universe of life, of love and the possibilities that that presents, and the way in which the church encompasses those possibilities. If there is a moral malaise in this country, in the West, the church is surely part of it; we have blessed it all, you see, and the way things are currently structured we have been ransomed by it. We are imprisoned in it. I agree with the vitriolic piece in the *Independent* the other day: the church has too many official privileges and institutional perks; we've effectively been ransomed by them, held in check.
>
> (Owen Jones 2000: 71)

An ironical future scenario presents itself where the Church of England finds its moral and spiritual freedom in disestablishment while person-centred therapy becomes a favoured part of the therapeutic establishment and loses its soul in a maze of NHS procedures and requirements. Unlikely as this scenario may be, it raises the spectre of a person-centred movement so determined to win legitimacy and a secure financial future for itself that it ceases to be a force for the spiritual evolution of humankind and becomes instead the lapdog of a dysfunctional society, subservient to its materialist ethic and no more than a half-hearted witness to the primacy of the inner life.

If this were to occur, although it would perhaps have the not inconsiderable merit of ensuring that many people would have access to some form of person-centred therapy to whom it would otherwise be denied, my fear is that the spiritual potency of the approach would be lost and with it the opportunity to be a truly prophetic force in the transformation of society. If the person-centred therapist with his or her commitment to full personhood, to unconditionality of love given and received and to the non-materialistic affirmation of the inner life bears the marks of a secular priesthood of the future, even more so does such commitment point to a prophetic

vocation with all the inevitable unpopularity which such a calling traditionally attracts.

In his last book, Carl Rogers, in what he described as a 'fragile' paper, took
on the role of prophet himself (Rogers 1980: 339–56). He attempted to draw
together what he saw as the developments in science, technology, parapsychology, education, psychotherapy and the study of ancient wisdom in order
to arrive at a vision of the future. He went further and conceptualized a
'person of tomorrow' in an attempt to predict the kind of human being who
would be able to live in a strange new world and would, indeed, play a major
part in shaping it. This vision was underpinned by Rogers' increasing conviction that there is what he called a 'formative tendency' at work in the cosmos
which can be observed at every level. He described it in a paper first delivered at a Theory Conference of the Association for Humanistic Psychology on
5 April 1975, which subsequently saw publication in 1978 (Rogers 1978).
The original presentation concluded, tentatively but clearly, with a statement
which, as far as I know, Rogers never retracted:

> It is hypothesized that there is a formative directional tendency in the universe,
> which can be traced and observed in stellar space, in crystals, in micro-organisms,
> in organic life, in human beings. This is an evolutionary tendency toward greater
> order, greater inter-relatedness, greater complexity. In humankind it extends from
> a single cell origin to complex organic functioning, to an awareness and sensing
> below the level of consciousness, to a conscious awareness of the organism and
> the external world, to a transcendent awareness of the unity of the cosmic system
> including man.
>
> (Rogers 1975: 6)

This is an immensely positive hypothesis for it postulates a tendency which is
stronger than the tendency toward deterioration or entropy as it is generally
known to physical scientists. There is an uncanny similarity with many
religious traditions (not least Christianity), which, while in no way denying
the reality of death, point to a life force which is greater than death and utterly
transformative. It is as if in this concept of the formative tendency Rogers the
empirical scientist, the psychotherapist and the mystic come together and
find in the work and writings of others the encouragement to continue their
collaboration. Such a holding of tensions is truly prophetic for it promises a
route towards the integration of science and religion which in turn heralds the
reconciliation and union of two modes of apprehending faith and meaning
which since the sixteenth century have been seen as mutually exclusive.

Rogers' depiction of the 'person of tomorrow' points to a world where
such a movement towards the reconciliation and union of science and
religion is well under way. Furthermore, there is at times a startling similarity
between the kind of priest portrayed in the diary of Peter Owen Jones and
the person described by Rogers as capable of living in tomorrow's world.

There is also, of course, the unspoken anxiety that without the emergence of such persons, tomorrow's world might never arrive at all. What is more, it does not take much imagination to grasp that any person-centred therapist who is bold enough to embrace such a way of being or to proclaim it as a model for others will receive a hostile reception in many quarters. The opposition, as Rogers himself suggested, is likely to be formidable but perhaps priests and prophets – whether religious or secular – should expect and even welcome conflict. Owen Jones, in one of his most bitter paragraphs, castigates the Church of England for standing 'resolutely against conflict'. He continues:

> There seems to be an overriding obsession to please, not to offend anyone – we have become soulless and saltless in the process. We are playing politicians' cards, but we are not politicians, we are priests; we govern nothing . . . Jesus Christ did not avoid conflict, he actually embraced it. He understood more than anyone that, by saying materialism, greed and sexual excess would not help you recognize how much you are loved by God, he would incur the wrath of those who were addicted to them. He left us with a blueprint for dealing with the conflict that will quite naturally arise when you stand up and say what he said.
>
> (Owen Jones 2000: 154)

It is perhaps salutary to conjecture what kind of conflict might ensue if a person-centred 'prophet' were to proclaim as necessary and desirable the characteristics of the 'person of tomorrow': I fantasise twelve new commandments based on Rogers' 'fragile' paper of 1980 and I deliver them with prophetic solemnity:

Be open to the world both inner and outer. Embrace and seek new experience, new ways of seeking and being, new ideas and new concepts.

Tell it the way it is. Reject hypocrisy, deceit and double talk. Be open about your relationships and your sexuality. Do not lead a secretive or double life.

Be deeply distrustful of our current science and the technology that is used to conquer the world of nature and to control the world's people.

Do not live in a compartmentalized world. Strive for a wholeness of life. Integrate the experience, thought, feeling, physical energy, psychic energy, healing energy.

Seek new forms of closeness, of intimacy and shared purpose. Seek new forms of communication both verbal and non-verbal, feelings and intellect.

Welcome risk-taking so that you may be vitally alive as you face change which is the only certainty of life.

Care for others with a gentle, subtle, nonmoralistic, nonjudgemental caring. Be suspicious of professional 'helpers'.

Feel close to and care for elemental nature. Be ecologically minded and ally
yourself with the forces of nature.

Distrust highly structured, inflexible, bureaucratic institutions. Remember
that institutions exist for people.

*Trust your own experience and be profoundly distrustful of external
authority.* Disobey laws you consider unjust.

Be indifferent to material comforts and rewards. Do not set your sights on
money or status symbols.

*Be spiritual seekers and find a meaning and purpose in life that is greater
than the individual.* Experience the unity and harmony of the universe.

(Based on Rogers 1980: 350–52)

It is not perhaps without significance that when Rogers came to name the
likely 'heroes' of his 'persons of tomorrow' he chose Mahatma Ghandi,
Martin Luther King and Teilhard de Chardin. It is difficult to imagine a more
spiritual and at the same time more socially engaged trio. Two were politicians as well as spiritual leaders, all three believed in the capacity of
humankind to evolve towards the light, two were assassinated and one
silenced. It would seem that if person-centred therapists are indeed to
become secular priests and prophets in a spiritually desperate and alienated
world they have no easy journey ahead. It is certain, too, that they will need
the companionship of all those other priests who, like Peter Owen Jones,
have discovered that priesthood transcends religious and credal boundaries
and in so doing ministers to the inner loneliness which, he declares, is
'ultimately a denial of soul . . . the greatest disease of our age'. It might also be
that person-centred secular priests and prophets would find themselves
saying of their way of life as Owen Jones says of his: 'it has surpassed all my
expectations' (Owen Jones 2000: 222). Whether they would be honoured
members of the psychotherapeutic establishment, however, is an altogether
different matter, and it is unlikely that they would be paying a higher rate of
income tax.

CHAPTER 5

The spiritual discipline of the person-centred therapist

In his discussion of the formative tendency, Rogers speaks of the human being's 'transcendent awareness of the unity of the cosmic system including man' (Rogers 1975: 6), and in his portrayal of the 'person of tomorrow' the climax is reached when he describes such persons as spiritual seekers who experience the unity and harmony of the universe (Rogers 1980: 352). For the person-centred therapist who conceptualizes his or her therapeutic work as essentially spiritual in nature, this emphasis on transcendent awareness and cosmic unity is of fundamental importance for it points to both a framework for and a guide to spiritual practice.

Profound spiritual experiences cannot be planned and predicted, and it would be foolish in the extreme to imagine that person-centred therapists can somehow be equipped to meet their clients in such a way that a transformational and transcendent experience is guaranteed. The knowledge, however, that a meeting in relational depth *can* lead to a sense of connectedness to the infinite resources of the cosmos certainly raises intriguing questions about the therapist's preparation and preparedness for such an eventuality. While it is clearly the case that grace cannot be compelled to come down, there is nevertheless an altogether valid question about what it is in a therapist that makes it more likely that such a powerful event will take place. Rogers had begun to hypothesize that the answer to this question lay in the quality of the therapist's 'presence' in the encounter. He even went so far as to suggest that such a quality constituted a powerful additional force to the attitudinal stance characterized by the core conditions of congruence, empathy and unconditional positive regard. At the same time he implied that without the prior establishment of the core conditions, such a quality of presence could not emerge – in a sense, then, it was the outcome of the experience by both client and therapist of the core conditions in their most intensive form which could lead to a breakthrough, however brief or temporary, into a transcendental or mystical state of consciousness where healing agents of great potency were released.

It could be argued that if the quality of presence is the outcome of the effective offering of the core conditions, the training and preparation of person-centred therapists need only seek to ensure that trainees are capable of consistently offering such conditions to their clients. The rest, as it were, can be left to the process with the expectation that sometimes grace will descend and sometimes not. I have much sympathy with this argument not least because, as we have seen, the task of embodying the core conditions is in itself a formidable one, and to expect more of trainees is altogether unreasonable. After all, they have not come for a training in spiritual development or in the cultivation of mystical awareness. Or have they? Here again, an apparently self-evident basic assumption needs questioning. If it is the case that person-centred therapy is open to the experience of the transcendent and if the offering of the core conditions is the prelude to such experience, then does it not follow that the person-centred therapist must do all that he or she can to be at home in the 'cosmic unity' where the visible and invisible worlds meet? Or, to put it another way, how can the person-centred therapist avoid the necessity of a spiritual discipline to equip him or her for such 'at homeness'?

Rogers' emphasis on the 'unity of the cosmic system' immediately suggests the underlying principle for such a spiritual discipline. Unity indicates a connectedness or relatedness between all things and all beings despite their self-evident differences and unique characteristics. A spirituality that is to do justice both to unity and to infinite diversity must find its strength in both the cultivation of respect for uniqueness and in the nurturing of an experienced connectedness. It follows therefore that there will be a paradox at the heart of a discipline which values in equal measure the uniqueness of the person and the wonder of relatedness. The person-centred therapist is at one and the same time both the sustainer of the individual's infinite worth (including his or her own) and the advocate of the interdependence of the whole created order. This is a spirituality which begins with an insistence on the absolute worth of the person and then extends this outwards to all that is. The anchorage in the self makes it possible for frail vessels to ride the storms of the cosmic ocean without the danger of total shipwreck. This inglorious metaphor attempts to convey something of the challenge that awaits the person-centred therapist who is courageous enough to accept the implications of working in a tradition which is wide open to 'transcendent awareness' and 'cosmic unity' while having its rootedness in the intimate relationship between two persons, one of whom is initially in a state of anxiety and incongruence.

The concept of self-love has been explored earlier and the potential for misunderstanding recognized as almost inevitable given the confusion with selfishness and the justifiable fear of self-inflation. And yet it is with self-love that the spiritual discipline of the person-centred therapist must begin, for without it the therapeutic enterprise is a charade where the therapist offers to the client an unconditionality of acceptance which he or she withholds from himself or herself. The ability to offer love to the self must often be fashioned on the anvil of suffering and guilt. There can be no pain greater than that of the self-loathing which springs from a sense of deep shame and unworthiness often engendered by the behaviour of others, who, in the worst instances, have been gross abusers and defilers. The spiritual discipline of self-love demands that the aspirant severs contact with such abusers – either temporarily or permanently – and assiduously seeks and fosters the companionship of those who, because of their own deep self-acceptance, can offer compassion, validation and a total absence of adverse judgement. Such a discipline – as with all disciplines – requires an act of will and of hope, for severing contact and seeking new companionship demand effort and energy which are often difficult to sustain.

A belief in an essentially affirming and cherishing heart to the cosmos – whether conceptualized as God or not – can be immensely comforting and supportive in such a search for new sources of validation. If I believe that God loves me, it makes it just that little more difficult for me to withhold love from myself for to do so is to suggest that God is squandering his love on a worthless being and, by implication, to throw it back in his face. Perhaps to reject the love of God or the benign energy of the cosmos is to inhabit the ultimate hell for it points to a self-loathing so deep that nothing can penetrate it. For the spiritual aspirant, however, no method must be left unexplored for searching out the heart of the cosmos and discovering its validating energy. Self-love is a moral imperative for the person-centred therapist and no potential path towards it must be neglected.

Sooner or later, in the quest for self-love, the body will demand attention. Indeed, for some it may constitute the first hurdle while for others it may be the last obstacle on the road. It is not without significance that for Adam and Eve in the ancient myth, their nakedness became a problem once they had ceased to trust God. Having eaten of the apple they could no longer face the divine presence in the Garden and became self-conscious and ashamed. Whether we like it or not we are embodied creatures and it is difficult to imagine how an attitude of self-love and self-acceptance could be established without being accompanied by a deep compassion for the body. It follows, then, that a spiritual discipline, if it is to be fully grounded, needs to encourage and strengthen a loving and compassionate response to the body. For the person-centred therapist this is of central importance for he or she is constantly exposed to the gaze of the client, and an ambivalence about the wholesomeness of physical being is quickly evidenced in gesture and other non-verbal behaviour. Clients who are in the presence of a therapist who is rejecting of his or her own body will at some level (which may be wholly conscious) receive the message that bodies are problematical and through this 'contamination effect' may well be reinforced in their rejection of their own physical beings. The person-centred therapist who wishes to convey acceptance to the client cannot afford to present a model of self-acceptance which is so visibly flawed, for if it is apparent that his or her body is not welcome in the therapist's own eyes it is difficult for the client to believe that an embracing self-love is ultimately possible.

A compassionate disposition towards the body has to be cultivated if it is not to remain a mere form of words or even an unwitting piece of self-deception. It is difficult to believe, for example, that a person is truly caring of his or her body if no attention is paid to diet or to the need for exercise and restorative sleep. A complete indifference to appearance is also difficult to equate with a real respect for the body and its manifestation in the world. To be dishevelled, unwashed or sporting food-stained or torn clothes scarcely suggests that the body is receiving the honour it deserves as the incarnation of personhood. The person-centred therapist who is concerned to honour his or her body will ponder these matters and will seek to translate into action a genuine response of concern and tenderness to the body which, after all, bears the task and the responsibility of carrying a person through life. For a person-centred therapist the weekly massage, the daily walk or run, the balanced diet may be an important part of a discipline which has at its heart a determination to live out an affirmation of the body's right to respect and compassion.

Such respect extends beyond a concern for health and appearance. Befriending the body involves also a willingness to listen to the messages which the body constantly attempts to convey. For the person-centred therapist such attentiveness is, in any case, a fundamental part of what it means to be congruent, to be in touch with the inner flow of experience. The body's pains, anxiety symptoms or intimations of joy and excitement provide a veritable kaleidoscope of impressions and messages which deserve to be heard. What Gendlin calls 'edge of awareness' feelings and experiences are a further extension of the data which the body can put at the disposal of the person who is genuinely respectful of the treasure house of which the body is the guardian. For some, the translation of such respect into practice may take the form of a daily period of meditative silence in which the body is allowed to speak its language without fear of interruption; for others it may involve a frequent attention to deep breathing which calms the body and allows it to locate its most important truths. Whatever the practice, the aim will be the same: to be deeply respectful of the body's wisdom and to attend to its messages, however unwelcome they may initially seem or however disruptive to the established order of things.

Compassion for the body will be a cornerstone of the person-centred therapist's spiritual discipline but so, too, will be an acceptant and empathic response to his or her inner world where conflicting voices and a confusing array of configurations may well be in residence. The person-centred therapist needs to be patient and unafraid of the family within, especially when they seem to be at each other's throats. The temptation for the therapist to ignore discordant inner voices or to refuse to acknowledge troublesome parts of himself or herself will be as great as it is for many clients. It is, after all, much simpler in the short run to filter out those tiresome aspects of the self which seem to impede clear-sightedness and a firm sense of direction. The spiritual discipline of the person-centred therapist should serve as a warning and as a defence against such wilful censoring. To encourage clients to be courageous in facing the seemingly conflicting aspects of their own being and to be equally attentive to them all will have about it a hollow ring if the therapist is intent on tuning out from certain of his or her own configurations because they are too inconvenient. Some therapists may have preserved the childhood ability to conduct vigorous group discussions with conflicting parts of the self and to emerge from such debate strengthened and invigorated. Many, however, will need to ensure that space is afforded in supervision for such work or that personal therapy is undertaken when inner conflict seems particularly ferocious. But whatever the method, the discipline is clear. The therapist's loving and respectful relationship with himself or herself must be a matter of high priority, and this must take full account of the body's need for affirmation and of the person's desire for empathic acceptance of his or her inner world with all its varied configurations and their apparently conflicting voices. The command 'Love yourself' (a part, incidentally, of the two great Christian commandments although seldom recognized as such) is not easily fulfilled, but for the person-centred therapist there is no legitimate escape from its stern but sweet demand.

The loving connectedness with the self is the prerequisite for the adventure of connecting with the other. The move into intimacy with all its inherent riskiness and challenge points to further aspects of the spiritual discipline which the person-centred therapist requires. Essentially it is a discipline which focuses on the nature of the other and draws from this the intuitive inspiration which makes for interpersonal connectedness at the deepest level. Unlikely as it may seem, the reference point for exploring the discipline which is required is the ideal relationship between two lovers. In the eyes of the lover, the beloved is beautiful and desirable: he or she is also sacred in the sense that no harm must occur for the beloved is worthy of the protection afforded to someone of infinite worth. The lover is energized by the presence of the beloved and is able to harness that energy, with all its inherent sexuality, so that the beloved experiences an enhancement of being in a climate of affirmation and absolute safety. The beloved feels deeply connected to the lover but is free and is in no way entrapped.

Sadly, few such ideal love relationships exist. All too often the lover is possessive and burns with a desire which casts little or no light. The beloved (either man or woman) often feels trapped or ensnared as well as flattered and affirmed. Sexuality is present but is often unharnessed and can become the source of destructiveness and fear rather than of ecstasy and transitory joy.

I would suggest that the ideal and seldom realized relationship between lovers can inform the person-centred therapist's spirituality of relationship and point to the discipline involved. There is about this discipline the cultivation of a profound faith both in the nature of personhood and in the transformational power of relationships. In pursuit of such faith the therapist will hold clients in his or her thoughts each day for a brief period – probably no more than a couple of minutes for each client – and the focus will be on both their current state of being and on their essential natures. This 'in-seeing' of clients will hold the visual image of their actual appearance in mind as a reference point while the eyes of faith will dwell on their inner beauty and resourcefulness, their sacredness and infinite worth. At the same time the therapist, while yearning for the client's good, imposes no direction upon the process and no pre-determined goal. This is a silent and passionate accompaniment without expectation but with absolute commitment to the client's evolution towards the fullness of being.

It is my contention – and experience – that the holding in mind of clients in this way on a regular basis can have a remarkable impact on the therapeutic relationship and its development. The ability of the therapist to be fully with the client is greatly enhanced as is the capacity for acceptance and validation. Furthermore, clients experience the therapist's commitment in a way which greatly increases their trust in themselves and the process.

This regular 'holding' of clients – in many ways much akin to silent or intercessory prayer – because it is part of a spiritual discipline is likely to have far-reaching effects in other areas of therapists' lives and to illumine all their relationships. The regular and systematic attentiveness to different levels of being makes for a perception of others which is not limited to that which is immediately observable or experienced. This results in a response which is both hopeful and affirming for it takes into account the individual as he or she is, but also conveys an appreciation and a sensing of all that he or she has it within them to become. This seeing with 'double vision' enables the observer to confer worth even when to all outward appearances there is little of worth to behold. The practice of the spiritual discipline leads to an attitudinal stance which – without effort – is exercised in all areas of the therapist's life. This does not mean that the therapist is never 'off duty'. Clearly, partners, family members, friends, acquaintances and work colleagues do not wish to be on the receiving end of persistent therapy, nor do the shop assistant or the postman require contrived doses of empathic acceptance. Their lives, however, will be enriched – sometimes even saved – by the presence of someone who endows them with value simply by virtue of a spontaneous respect conveyed by a smile, a gesture or a courteous word. In person-centred terms, those who exercise such a way of being in the world bear witness to the power of the facilitative relationship and to a belief in the resilience of the actualizing tendency. They are making a statement about the essential wonder of the human person and about the affirming potential of human connectedness. In this sense, they are beacons of hope and their spiritual discipline enables them to become this without self-consciousness and without prodigious efforts of the will.

If the attitude to the self and to others constitutes a major and, in many ways, logical agenda for the person-centred therapist, it is perhaps less obvious that the response to the whole created order is supremely relevant to those who aspire to 'experience the unity and harmony of the universe'. At a period in human history when anxiety about the future of the planet mounts alarmingly almost from week to week, there is no issue of greater urgency. Compassionate engagement with the suffering earth and an identification with the beauty of creation become poignant areas for the person-centred therapist's spiritual agenda. There is, too, a need to honour the fruits of human creativity where they nourish the yearning for the transcendent and offer release from alienation. It is to my mind self-evident that therapists who are intent upon creating a climate for growth for their clients need to be particularly attentive not only to the interpersonal climate of their own lives but also to the context of their natural environment and of their intellectual and aesthetic world. A spiritual discipline which takes these issues seriously will seek to ensure that the therapist is not divorced from nature and is constantly nourished by the best which human creativity has to offer. For my part, I count it essential that I visit the sea frequently, that I train my eye to observe the intricate designs of trees and plants and that I make friends with animals. What is more, I am horrified if I discover that I have let a whole week go past without having read a poem, listened to music, visited a beautiful building or feasted my eyes on a work of art. I know that I need to do these things if I am to cultivate a sense of my deep connectedness to all that is, and – most importantly – if I am to retain a sense of awe and wonder at the marvels of creation whether natural or human.

Perhaps it is this sense of awe and wonder which is, in the end, the most precious outcome of the spiritual discipline which the person-centred therapist can choose to embrace. Such a sense preserves an openness to be surprised by the resourcefulness and beauty of the human being and of the natural world. It can also lead to a trust in the infinite resourcefulness of the invisible world. It is at this point that the person-centred pragmatists are likely to back off in despair at the final descent into 'new-agery' and into the mystical talk which they fear will ensure that person-centred therapy is condemned to the same rubbish bin where the most dubious of the 'alternative therapies' are deposited.

Rogers, however, gave embarrassing evidence of a willingness to explore the invisible world, which it is difficult for the pragmatists to acknowledge, let alone to take seriously. His excursions into parapsychology after his wife, Helen's, death is but one example of a curiosity which pushed him to move beyond the conventional boundaries of the day-to-day world. His reference to the 'something larger' which entered into the picture when he was able to be fully present to the other in a therapeutic relationship is perhaps the most striking indication of his belief in untapped resources which are, presumably, ever around us but denied to our experience unless we are fully present to ourselves and to others. It is important to emphasize again that for Rogers such an emerging belief was not the outcome of wild speculation but of his experience with individuals and in groups. The heightened consciousness which occurred from time to time in those contexts, characterized by a depth of relating which transcended time and space, led him to conclude that 'something larger' was being accessed.

My own experience points to an additional dimension to these experiences. I have discovered that it is often when my client and I have come to accept our powerlessness to change things and are content to dwell in our relationship without expectation that new possibilities emerge. It is as if a combination of accepted powerlessness, deep relationship and waiting without expectation open up a channel into new terrain where help is at hand. If I am to take such experiences seriously – and I do because they are not infrequent and others report similar occurrences – it follows that the spiritual discipline of the person-centred therapist should also encourage me in this waiting without expectation and in a preparedness to accept powerlessness as a mark of my hope and not of my despair. What such a discipline might mean for a given therapist is clearly dependent on many factors, not least the therapist's personality and other belief and value systems which the therapist embraces. The task, however, will be the same – to cultivate a willingness to let go into powerlessness as a positive response to difficulty and confusion and to wait patiently for the invisible world to reveal its treasures whether through thoughts or feelings or the intervention of unexpected external forces. This clearly entails the systematic setting aside of time so that such openness to the invisible world can be developed and sustained. This is an altogether different exercise to the attentive response to the body described earlier, for it is a waiting which fosters a deep receptivity to the forces of creativity, love and healing. For me, as a Christian, the obvious setting is that of the Eucharist where I am required to still myself and to enter into a mystery where I am invited to be the recipient of the 'food of heaven' and to join my fellow human-beings, the angels and the saints as I do so. The visible and the invisible worlds meet and my task is to be the one who waits, powerless and without expectation but in silent hope. For the atheist or agnostic or those of other faiths I have no doubt that there are many ways which can be devised to encourage the same letting go so that the invisible world can reveal its treasures to the one who is prepared to acknowledge powerlessness and to wait without expectation but without despair.

It will be clear by now that the person-centred therapist who wishes to take his or her spiritual responsibilities seriously has, as I perceive it, an arduous formation to undertake. Nothing that I have proposed here in any way negates the necessity for good supervision in the conventional sense. Spirituality can easily become an escape route and even a defence against self-exploration. The person-centred therapist needs to ensure that his or her supervisor cannot unwittingly be manipulated by 'spiritual' posturing or practices which are, in effect, an evasion of the interpersonal dynamics of a therapeutic relationship or a denial of the therapist's need to face his or her own fears and anxieties. Nor does the spiritual dimension of the therapist's work diminish the need for close collegial support. Those who belong to various faith communities have the 'sounding board' of the community and its traditions and teachings as some defence against self-deception and self-inflation, and to be without such a 'monitoring' influence can place the therapist in a potentially dangerous and vulnerable position. Person-centred therapists, perhaps more than therapists from some other traditions, need their colleagues to sustain them and help them guard against power-trips or burnouts, and those who engage with the spiritual struggles of their clients and are not themselves accompanied on their spiritual journeys will do well to be highly attentive to their need for support and containment.

With all these necessary caveats, however, there is no escaping the stern and inescapable fact that spiritual work requires spiritual discipline. The person-centred practitioner must find a way of cultivating such a discipline so that it 'fits' both his or her personality and beliefs, and the practice of a secular therapy which assiduously avoids the imposition of direction or 'revealed truth' on clients. I have attempted to show what such a discipline might look like with its various emphases on the body, the inner world of the therapist, the cultivation of 'double vision' in the sustaining of relationships, the cherishing of the natural world and of human creativity and, finally, the patient waiting upon the invisible world. Such a discipline will, I believe, do much to equip the therapist in his or her desire to be fully present to clients in such a way that the movement into an altered state of consciousness, where 'something larger' enters in and potent healing forces are released, is the more likely. It may well be that grace cannot be commanded to come down but at least we can do our bit to ensure that we are in a state of readiness for its arrival. 'What,' it may be asked, 'is grace anyway?' – and the very question reveals how blurred is the boundary between the secular and the sacred in the practice of person-centred therapy as I have come to experience it. Perhaps the spiritual discipline which I am commending sees that blurring not as an unfortunate confusion but as the beginnings of a new integration of worlds whose separation has brought the planet to the verge of catastrophe.

So solemn a chapter as this needs to end on an altogether lighter and more reassuring note. Any attempt to offer guidelines for a spiritual discipline inevitably runs the risk of sounding prescriptive and even doctrinaire. What is more it can induce in the potential aspirant a sense of anxiety or even hopelessness at the thought of having to attain to such heights of apparent integration and spiritual perfection. Person-centred therapists, fortunately, are all too human, and I am the first to acknowledge that I have feet of clay and often fall far short of the counsel of perfection which this chapter may seem to offer. When that happens – as it invariably does – I have to exercise an even sterner discipline and remind myself with all the passion I can muster that person-centred therapy is built on the corner stone of unconditional positive regard. If any so-called spiritual discipline leads me to feel self-denigratory, guilt-ridden or just plain incompetent, better that I abandon such a discipline and simply affirm my imperfect and wounded humanity as more than good enough.

CHAPTER 6

Person-centred therapy: a key to the resolution of three intractable conflicts

When I am tempted to despair and to give up hope for the future of humankind, it is often because I see little chance of resolving three major conflicts which threaten the continuation of our life together on planet earth. I am, of course, disturbed that these conflicts seem not to be so palpably obvious nor their implications so terrifying to everyone else. It is difficult to believe that I am the only sighted person in a land of the blind and in my more sane moments I know that this cannot possibly be the case. And yet it is difficult to avoid the feeling that I am being naïve and singularly unsophisticated when I take the risk of naming these conflicts. The first is that between global commercialization and ecological survival, the second that between science and religion and the third the continuing conflict between the great religions of the world.

In Chapter 4 I fantasized twelve new 'commandments' based on Rogers' vision of the 'person of tomorrow', and it is perhaps not surprising, as we shall see, that several of them address precisely the conflict areas to which I have just alluded. My despair at the first conflict is fuelled when I am confronted by the stark realization that commerce and the demands of the global economy seem to take precedence in the minds of politicians and government leaders over all else. Currently in Britain, for example, thousands of animals are being slaughtered (both sick and healthy) because the world-wide demand for cheap food is apparently absolute. (The severe outbreak of foot and mouth disease in the UK in 2001 has revealed starkly that farming is a ruthless industry and animals merely a source of profit.) In our schools and colleges young people are subjected to an overly materialistic and mechanistic educational experience because this is deemed necessary if 'standards' are to be 'raised' so that Britain may achieve a leading role in the global economy. The levels of distress which such a blinkered policy is inflicting on pupils and teachers alike are either ignored or seen as an acceptable cost to be paid for the 'modernization' of the educational system. Again, the appalling dependence on the motor car continues unabated because the economic and political implications of curtailing such dependence are apparently unmanageable or unthinkable. In the face of such a world, Rogers' 'person of tomorrow' is challenged to care for elemental nature while being indifferent to material comforts and rewards. This is a 'counter-cultural' manifesto with radical implications. To take it seriously would mean for most of us a conversion signalling demands way beyond any conventional religious observance.

Much of modern science and technology serves to underpin this economic imperialism which currently brooks no opposition. Throughout the world it is big business which increasingly funds scientific research and dictates its fields of enquiry. With such obsequiousness before the altar of materialism it is scarcely surprising that science, ambivalent at best, is becoming increasingly antagonistic to the claims of religion, whose 'irrationalism' and commitment to unprovable beliefs is increasingly ridiculed. Those scientists – particularly physicists and biologists – who continue to embrace religious belief are often seen as having forfeited an honoured place in the scientific community. In the face of such increasing divisiveness, the challenge to the 'person of tomorrow' speaks again with the voice of a profoundly subversive counter-culture: 'Be deeply distrustful of our current science and the technology that is used to conquer the world of nature and to control the world's people.'

Sadly, the present state of relationships between the world's great religions scarcely provides a more hopeful backdrop. Although there have been some remarkable developments in inter-faith dialogue, most notably between Christians, Hindus and Buddhists (e.g. Griffiths 1989) and some public manifestations of inter-faith solidarity (for example, the coming together of the world's religious leaders to pray for peace at Assisi on Pope John Paul's invitation in 1986), the situation worldwide remains bleak. Jews and Arabs continue in bitter conflict in the Middle East; Moslem and Christian remain at murderous loggerheads in Serbia and Macedonia; Hindus, Moslems and Christians often fail to maintain an uneasy co-existence in India and Pakistan, while in Africa countless inter-racial and religious conflicts fuel permanent unrest. Within the Christian churches themselves, the age-old battles between Catholic, Protestant and Orthodox are by no means dead as current situations in Ireland, Russia and the Balkan states only too tragically bear witness. In the face of such bitter feuding and deep-rooted antagonism, the person of tomorrow is nonetheless challenged to be a spiritual seeker and to find a meaning and purpose in life that is greater than the individual. Once again, Carl Rogers has left a prophetic legacy which seeks to address the very conflicts which threaten to destroy civilization as we have known it.

Not for the first time in the writing of this book, I am filled with an uneasy sense of pushing things too far. It is one thing to claim for person-centred therapy a possible response to the mystical yearnings of many twenty-first-century secular men and women, but it is altogether more grandiose to suggest that this therapeutic approach has within it the seeds of harmonious reconciliation between science and religion and between the world's great faiths. To suggest that it may also illuminate and thus help to avert the ultimate folly of unbridled materialism is perhaps the final sign of a desire to claim for the approach and for Rogers a place in the story of human evolution which cannot possibly be justified. At such a moment and in order to temper my embarrassment I remind myself that the person of tomorrow is also challenged to trust his or her own experience and to be profoundly distrustful of external authority. What is more, there is the invitation to embrace new ways of seeking and being and to discover fresh ideas and new concepts. With such encouragement, I propose to accept the risk of being considered foolishly misguided as I attempt to explore further how person-centred theory and practice could hold the key to unlocking these areas of potentially lethal conflict.

My starting point is the untapped resource of empathy. The ability to enter another's frame of reference and to see and experience the world as he or she sees and experiences it is, in fact, a most revolutionary activity. It immediately renders difference challenging rather than threatening and offers the possibility of communion rather than estrangement. To be an empathic person holds out the hope of meeting. Of course, empathic skill can be most cruelly abused, for to understand another person in depth is to be in a position to manipulate, to exploit and even to destroy. When empathy is allied, however, to a genuine desire to accept the other person, then an altogether different process becomes possible. Person-centred theory with its emphasis on the inter-relatedness of empathy, acceptance and congruence guards against a facile cultivation of empathy which, on its own, can just as well lead to malevolent exploitation as to compassionate accompaniment. Unscrupulous salespeople often possess – and have been trained to possess – considerable empathic ability and as a result can persuade their beguiled victims to purchase what in their right mind they would never dream of buying. Given this vital caveat, it is clear from thera-peutic experience that empathic responsiveness can result in profound healing which gives back to people a sense of belonging to the human race. Put simply, empathy can be marvellously restorative. It has the capacity to heal inner conflicts as well as to bring about understanding between persons who are in bitter conflict with each other – the even-handed empathic responsiveness of the person-centred family therapist provides a powerful example of the latter (O'Leary 1999). The important requirement, however, is that the empathy is firmly anchored in a deeply authentic and acceptant regard for the other.

Let me not draw back from expressing clearly my outrageous hypothesis. It is this: if the world were populated by large numbers of empathic people whose empathy was anchored in a deep acceptance of self and others and in an authenticity based on profound self-awareness, then materialism would gradually lose its stranglehold, science and religion would make friends together and the world faiths would be united in their spiritual quest. Divisiveness and hostility would give place to cooperation and communion. This is self-evidently an idealistic vision of an earthly paradise. My point is that without such a vision, however unattainable, we may well be a doomed species. It is worth giving it our best shot for, as the Hebrew prophet tells us, where there is no vision the people assuredly perish.

In my university we are currently preparing ourselves for the visit of a group of Japanese person-centred practitioners, scholars and trainees. It is a matter of considerable interest and no little surprise that almost all of Carl Rogers' work has been translated into Japanese. On the face of it, Japanese culture would not seem to offer the most congenial home for person-centred ideas and practice. Both the social mores and the spiritual tradition of Japan are far removed from the American and European contexts where the approach has developed. Such an analysis, however, does not penetrate beneath the surface. The fact that Rogers' influence on some Japanese psychotherapists has been profound and that person-centred practice and theory are once more gaining ground points to a much deeper level of spiritual convergence. This becomes apparent when we focus again on the intense and transformational moments of the therapeutic encounter. Rogers' claim that at such moments an altered state of consciousness gives access to a transcendental realm where 'something larger' enters in is taken up by the Japanese scholar, Yoshihiko Morotomi, but leads to surprisingly different insights. For Westerners, the encounter gives rise to a miracle of relationship where the level of mutual engagement reveals an intensity of connectedness with all that is. To experience such mystical communion through relationship is to gain a new perspective which can render life's sufferings and difficulties of little or no account. For Morotomi, however, the implications of the encounter are somewhat different. Following in the tradition of Fujio Tomoda (1967), Morotomi sees the encounter at its most sublime moments as making it possible for the client to enter the 'vacuum' where he or she experiences total aloneness (Morotomi 1998). The relationship enables the client to surrender all the psychological and emotional anxieties and disturbances which normally cloud his or her mind and heart. It is the empathic companion who receives them and thereby frees the client to be totally alone so that the journey inward can be pursued without hindrance. In a paradoxical way, the relationship at its best becomes the prerequisite for the aloneness which makes spiritual growth possible.

These two reflections on the same order of experience point to the remarkable capacity of the person-centred approach to transcend cultural boundaries and to initiate dialogue between different spiritual traditions. Fujio Tomoda is a Buddhist, and in the Zen tradition the realization of the true self is identical with the realization of absolute Nothingness. The 'vacuum' and the total aloneness to which person-centred therapy gives access can therefore be seen as essential features of the spiritual path which leads to a liberation and detachment from all things and where ego is eliminated. The true self, as Morotomi puts it, awakens to itself and every form of subject–object duality is transcended. To put it another way, the experience of person-centred therapy can become for the Zen Buddhist the means whereby the gradual self-awakening takes place which leads to freedom and detachment from every kind of trouble and suffering.

For the Westerner, the intensity of relationship is experienced differently. It is the deep sense of communion which enables both client and therapist to transcend their normal ego states with all their accompanying anxieties and preoccupations. It is as if the one person needs the other in order to be free to achieve full selfhood. The paradox here, however, is that the relationship leads to self-forgetfulness and not to self-inflation. It is not difficult to see this way of interpreting experience as wholly aligned with the Christian tradition with its emphasis on the love of neighbour as oneself and the mystical indwelling of Christ as the true life force. When as a therapist I am fully present to my client and 'something larger' enters in, then we are both, in Christian terminology, living the life of Christ within us and our suffering is placed in a new perspective. To put it another way, the experience of person-centred therapy can become for the Christian the means whereby the second great commandment is vibrantly enacted and access is afforded to the living God within both persons and, by extension, within all that is.

The Buddhist and Christian ways of understanding the richness of the person-centred encounter at its most heightened intensity point to an intriguing possibility. It is increasingly clear that there is little likelihood of the world's great religious traditions finding much more than limited common ground if the search is confined to doctrinal or even mytho-poetic exploration. It is self-evident that the belief systems, while having some elements in common, diverge widely in many important respects. If it were not so, it would be difficult to understand why so much blood has been spilt and so many wars fought in the name of holy religion. The fact that the person-centred experience of relational depth lends itself to different but compatible interpretations based on Western and Eastern spiritual traditions suggests an altogether more hopeful way forward. It would seem that when we bypass doctrine and mythological themes and focus instead on the contemplative core of all religions, the picture is very different. The mystical experience and the transcendental consciousness which it inspires point to a commonality which can unite rather than divide. The ways of understanding the experience may vary and the interpretation in cognitive terms take a different shape, but the experience itself is susceptible to enquiry and constitutes what we might term the essential heart and soul of religious faith. The intriguing possibility is that a secular therapeutic tradition, once it fully acknowledges the mystical realm to which its practice gives access, may serve as a bridge between the great faith traditions and enable them to converse creatively together not about their doctrinal differences, which can seem intractable, but about the direct spiritual experience inherent in the contemplative core which lies at the heart of all of them. Perhaps it is for this reason that, at the present time, inter-faith dialogue shows its most hopeful face when it is engaged upon by monks and nuns who have committed themselves to deep contemplation and who therefore meet not to debate doctrine but to share their contemplative experience, which often defies immediate expression. In this sense they are challenged to articulate the inexpressible and to forge a language and a mode of communication which can do justice to precisely that experience which gives meaning and sustaining energy to their lives.

Perhaps the notion of person-centred therapy as a facilitative force in the crucial task of inter-faith dialogue is a wild flight of fancy on my part. The idea becomes much less absurd, however, when we remember that person-centred therapy has itself developed a view of the person and of human relating based on clinical practice and rigorous empirical enquiry which has then, in turn, given rise to the not infrequent experience, both in one-to-one encounters and in groups, of a dimension of being for which language is inadequate and to which Rogers himself – with extreme reluctance – could only apply such words as spiritual, mystical and transcendent. It is as if without seeking it and almost in spite of itself, a secular therapy – originated by a psychologist and his colleagues who prided themselves on being empirical scientists – has stumbled upon a dimension of experience which cannot be denied and for which the usual language of psychology and therapeutic discourse is ill-equipped and inappropriate. Seen in this light the thought of secular therapists becoming the facilitators of communication between the religions of the world is not so totally fanciful. Once it becomes possible for person-centred practitioners to acknowledge that, whether they like it or not, they are spiritual or existential explorers by virtue of the terrain to which their practice gives access, then it does not require too great a leap to reach the point of offering deep respect and empathy to those in all the great religions of the world who struggle to articulate and to live out the implications of their direct mystical experiences. The tragedy would be great indeed if person-centred therapists refused to acknowledge the nature of the terrain to which their commitment to relational depth gives access, or if they were so blinded and angered by the destructive effects of religious bigotry and doctrinal straitjackets that they could not perceive the heart, soul and essence of religion which is manifest in the experience of the mystic of all the great world faiths. Sadly, there is much evidence to suggest that both of these tragic possibilities could come about. There are, as we have seen, those person-centred practitioners who would prefer that Carl Rogers had neither undergone nor written about his spiritual and mystical experiences as a therapist and group facilitator and thereby, in their estimation, sullied his reputation as an empirical scientist and clinician. There are also many in the ranks of the person-centred community who, like Rogers himself, have suffered grievously at the hands of punitive and life-denying religious beliefs and practices. Their hatred and legitimate fury at the savage wounds inflicted upon them by the representatives of such perverse religion make it difficult and, in some cases, well-nigh impossible for them to believe that there are those in the ranks of the religious believers with whom they could converse as friends and fellow seekers. Indeed, for such believers, sustained as they are by the deepest experiences of their mystical journey, the secular person-centred therapist, free of all the trappings of institutional and doctrinal religion, is likely to be a more congenial companion and soul-friend than the co-religionist who has never penetrated to the heart of the faith he or she professes to practise.

It is the formidable Ken Wilber who has seen that it is the direct mystical core of all religions that also has within it the hope of reconciliation between science and religion. His reflections on this possible route towards the resolution of the conflict which has beset humankind for at least the last three centuries again raise intriguing questions about the role that person-centred therapy might find itself playing in such a process of reconciliation. In *The Marriage of Sense and Soul* (Wilber 1998), Wilber argues with his usual passion and logical clear-sightedness that if religion and science are ever to join hands, religion must be able to pass the test of what he calls 'deep science'. He sees this test as exemplifying three essential aspects of scientific enquiry, which he names instrumental injunction, direct apprehension and communal confirmation. Simply put, this constitutes the process of doing something (an experience, an actual practice), the direct and immediate experience resulting from the doing (the experiential data), and the checking of the result with others who have similarly carried out the experiment and possess the experiential data. Wilber continues his argument by stating bluntly that when we come to consider the great religions of the world there is no way forward for scientific enquiry, thus construed, if attention is confined to doctrinal formulations or mythological themes. It is only in the study of the direct spiritual experience inherent in the contemplative core of all religions that the test of 'deep science' can be realistically applied. If such a test can successfully be undertaken it is Wilber's belief that 'religion can both stand up to modernity and offer something for which modernity has desperate need: a genuine, verifiable, respectable injunction to bring forth the spiritual domain' (Wilber 1998: 167).

Wilber's reflections, which have for me the power of inspirational insight, throw light on the role that psychotherapy – and person-centred therapy in particular – may have to play in resolving the conflict between science and religion. What is more the process of Carl Rogers' own life and work exemplifies the direction of such possible reconciliation. More perhaps than most transpersonal psychologists and therapists, Rogers moved from the position of the empirical scientist to that of the spiritual seeker without ever abandoning his passionate commitment to empirical enquiry. From the outset he was determined to subject the interpersonal processes of the therapeutic relationship to the rigorous test of scientific scrutiny. Unlike those therapists – particularly of the psychoanalytical school – who believed that to bring scientific methodology to bear on the interaction between therapist and client was somehow improper and potentially harmful, Rogers showed himself determined not to divorce profound human experiencing from the scientific analysis which was for him an equally important aspect of the human enterprise. It was for him a matter of regret that in the time prior to his death there were as yet no valid empirical methods for exploring the mystical and transcendent experiences which had become such an important part of his personal and professional life. His enthusiastic reception of the emerging methods of qualitative research leave little doubt, however, that, had he lived longer, the application of what Wilber calls 'deep science' to the mystical moments of the therapeutic encounter would have become for him an increasingly urgent priority. His encouragement to Maria Bowen, one of his most loved and admired colleagues, to pursue her study of intuition in therapy is a further indication of the importance he had attached to holding in creative tension the courage to be and the passion to understand (Bowen 1986). His response to Maria is a particularly moving example not only of his deep respect for perhaps the most 'mystical' of his associates but also of his desire to honour equally the mystic and the empirical scientist in himself. If the mystical experience is seen as the core of the religious quest, there can be no doubt that Carl Rogers remains a pioneer in the task of resolving the conflict between science and religion, and heralds the time when they at last enter upon an era of co-operative dialogue in the interest of the future survival of humankind and of the planet. The awesome thought is that for the international person-centred community the responsibility for taking our part in and sustaining such co-operation may already be upon us.

CHAPTER 7

The use of self

In the last year of his life Carl Rogers gave a remarkable interview to Michèle Baldwin on the use of self in therapy. It would seem that Rogers was in a particularly expansive mood, and although he could not have known it at the time, the interview is in many ways his final testimony. In it he reviews many aspects of his professional life but, more significantly, he offers a number of provocative statements about his current thinking and feeling on a number of central issues, including his view of spiritual reality (Baldwin 2000).

He begins by recalling his relationship with a schizophrenic man in Wisconsin. The climactic point in the relationship was when Rogers, faced with the man's despair and his indifference to whether he lived or died, said, 'I realize that you don't care about yourself, but I want you to know that I care about you and I care what happens to you'. The effect on the man was instantaneous and he broke into sobs for ten or fifteen minutes. The therapy then took an altogether more positive turn. Rogers ponders on this incident and reflects that it was when he came to the man 'as a person' and expressed his feelings for him that a real impact was made. This, in turn, prompts Rogers to wonder whether in his writings he had perhaps 'stressed too much the three basic conditions of congruence, unconditional positive regard and empathic understanding'. 'Perhaps,' he says, 'it is something round the edges of those conditions that is really the most important element of therapy – when my self is very clearly, obviously present' (Baldwin 2000: 30).

There are many other instances in this interview when Rogers seems to be throwing caution to the winds and expresses with great forcefulness ideas and perceptions which would find little place in the conventional arenas of counselling and psychotherapy. Indeed, Rogers acknowledges readily that academic circles can accommodate his viewpoints only with great difficulty. His earlier work, he believes, was acceptable to the cognitive, academic mind, but 'what has been happening since' can find no place in the major universities where people are not even willing to try to understand his work.

In essence, Rogers repeatedly affirms in this interview that it is who the therapist is, how fully he or she can invest himself or herself in the moment and how secure he is in his own being that matters. Such security does not imply invulnerability. On the contrary, to be accessible to another, it is important to acknowledge imperfection and flaws, and Rogers goes so far as to say that the very ability to help at all depends on such an acknowledgement. He goes on to speak of relationships where a level of such intimacy and intensity is reached that he feels his simple presence is healing. He concludes that it is because of the state of his own being in such instances that immense energy is released which flows from him to the client. These are, in fact, astonishing claims and could justifiably attract accusations of arrogance and of self-inflation. Rogers goes further. He claims unambiguously that there are times that 'the best of therapy . . . leads to a dimension that is spiritual' (Baldwin 2000: 35). At such times there comes a meeting of inner spirit with inner spirit and the experience of being part of 'something larger'. It is, of course, an unwritten subtext that such experiences are powerfully beneficial to the client as well as involving the therapist in a process which is transformational.

In the context of such frankly mystical reflections, it is perhaps not surprising that Rogers, not for the first time, inveighs against psychoanalysts and the reliance on the concept of transference. Essentially he sees the notion of the transference as a hugely sophisticated device for preventing true relationship and for defending the therapist against real involvement where the exploration of the actual feelings between two persons can take place. It is not going too far to say that Rogers' anger with psychoanalysis sprang both from his belief that it almost guaranteed inauthenticity and from his increasing perception in his later years that it prevented access to the spiritual terrain.

Throughout the interview with Michèle Baldwin, Rogers comes across as someone liberated from the shackles of the world of professional psychology. What is more – as in his comments about the core conditions – he seems increasingly willing to sit lightly to his own previous theoretical constructs. He is a man who, in his 85th year and with nothing to lose, dares to utter what previously he might have feared would be ridiculed and laughed out of court. It is also perhaps significant that he is not having to go through the highly conscious process of producing his own manuscript; instead he lets himself relax in a conversation with an exceptionally facilitative female interviewer. The brakes are off and the words come tumbling out with a fluency and an abandon which are exhilarating. It would seem that Rogers the academic and Rogers the empirical scientist – although frequently glimpsed in the background – have for the moment been sent on holiday. Almost guiltily, however, it is at the very point when he is struggling to articulate his spiritual experiences that Rogers reminds himself and his interviewer that he is, after all, a scientist as well as a mystic: 'Sometimes I feel much as the physicists, who do not really split atoms; they simply align themselves up in accordance with the natural way in which the atoms split themselves. In the same way, I feel that sometimes in interpersonal relationships power and energy get released which transcends what we thought was involved' (Baldwin 2000: 36).

It would seem that the holiday for the scientist and academic is more illusory than real, but it is also clear that Rogers, in this final interview, is at pains to embrace a science which can contribute to the study of direct spiritual experience in the way envisioned by Ken Wilber in his quest for reconciliation between science and religion. Some years previously Rogers had already begun to sketch out the terrain when in *A Way of Being* he had written enthusiastically about the work of the theoretical physicist, Fritjof Capra, and the chemist-philosopher, Ilya Prigogine (Rogers 1980: 130–31). Prigogine's work on systems of energy within the environment, with its suggestion that the world of nature is 'probabilistic rather than solely deterministic', was, for Rogers, nothing short of inspirational. Prigogine maintained that the more complex a structure became, the more energy it expended to maintain its complexity and this made for an essentially creative instability. For Rogers, this made sense of transformational states in the human being and why it was that many factors acting on one another at once could lead to psychological shifts and physiological changes of profound importance. He linked this to Gendlin's concept of 'experiencing' in psychotherapy (Gendlin 1978) and found in Prigogine's ideas support for the efficacy of 'perturbing' a system through the full recognition and expression of previously withheld or suppressed feelings. For Rogers, Prigogine's work and that of other cutting-edge scientists held out the promise of a humanity truly capable of self-transcendence. Nor was it unimportant that Prigogine saw in his 'science of complexity' a strong resemblance with the discoveries of 'Eastern sages and mystics' (Rogers 1980: 132).

In the pages of *A Way of Being* we detect Rogers' excitement as he discovers in unexpected quarters the validation of experiences which he had been forced to acknowledge as a therapist and group facilitator and which had previously eluded rational explanation. What was undeniable, however, was the potency of such experiences and their transformational effect upon those undergoing them. Prigogine and Capra brought comfort to the empirical scientist in Rogers because they pointed to a science which could grapple with phenomena which he had previously labelled 'transcendent', 'indescribable', 'unexpected' and 'transformational'. In a sense, they made it 'respectable' for him to be a mystic. What is more, they provided scientific support for his ever-hopeful view of humanity because they pointed to an evolutionary potential which was life-affirming. At the end of Chapter 6 of *A*

Way of Being he dares to express clearly what was, in essence, the justifica-tion of his life's work: '. . . perhaps we are touching the cutting edge of our ability to transcend ourselves, to create new and more spiritual directions in human evolution' (Rogers 1980: 134).

For Rogers the ability to be fully himself in his relationships, to let himself be, was clearly aided by the scientific underpinning afforded to transcend-ental experience by such scientists as Capra and Prigogine. Bergin, in an article published in *American Psychologist* in 1991, refers to a letter, received from Rogers in 1985, which shows just how far such scientific support had emboldened him: 'I do believe there is some kind of transcend-ent organizing influence in the universe which operates in man as well . . . my present very tentative view (of humans) is that perhaps there is an essen-tial person which persists through time, or even through eternity' (Bergin 1991: 394). One clear implication of such a statement is that Rogers was prepared to face the possibility that both he and his client – together with all humanity – might be living 'sub specie aeternitatis' with all the immense implications of such a possibility for an understanding of the self and its evolution. It is clear, however, from the interview with Michèle Baldwin that Rogers, whatever solidarity he might feel with such scientists as Capra and Prigogine, did not expect similar support from fellow psychologists. It is diffi-cult to avoid the conclusion that during the last years of his life he felt increas-ingly alienated from the profession which in his early days he had so strongly defended against the aggressive stance of psychiatric medicine. When he went to Wisconsin in 1957 as Professor both of Psychology and Psychiatry he could scarcely have imagined that some years later it would be the Chair of Psychology which he would relinquish as a protest against the narrow-minded and power-seeking attitudes of his psychological colleagues. The increasing disenchantment with psychology is plain when in his discussion of the training of therapists he says to Baldwin: 'I'd rather have someone who read widely and deeply in literature or in physics, than to have someone who has always majored in psychology in order to become a therapist. I think that breadth of learning along with breadth of life experience are essential to becoming a good therapist' (Baldwin 2000: 37). The scarcely veiled implica-tion is that neither breadth of learning nor breadth of life experience would be in any way guaranteed by the study of psychology.

For Rogers, the ability to be 'very clearly, obviously present' in his relation-ships – an ability which, as we have seen, he was beginning to suspect was the essential element in therapy, more important even than the presence of the core conditions – was not easily sustained. In the interview with Baldwin the very complexity of such an ability becomes evident. The criteria of openness to experience, inner security, vulnerability, acknowledgement of flaws and imperfection, the capacity to be in the moment, the commitment to empowering others, the belief in the constructive core of the person – all these are familiar from much of Rogers' writing and constitute a formidable challenge in themselves. What perhaps is new in this interview, however, is the emphasis on 'letting go of yourself', surrendering to a process, being confident enough to proceed without complete understanding knowing that it is possible to 'come back' to oneself. Furthermore, it is evident that for Rogers such self-surrender – seen as the ultimate 'use' of the self – can only be undertaken by someone who has a 'breadth of learning' and a 'breadth of life experience'. I would suggest that this requirement, expressed with somewhat uncharacteristic emphasis by Rogers, is saying something of the utmost import-ance about a therapist's total *Weltanschauung*. The ability to surrender the self, but also to return to it, demands trustworthy reference points in the vast terrain of an evolutionary world in which the person is himself or herself a changing element of self-transcendent potential. For Rogers, it would seem that, as an empirical scientist, such reference points were provided by pioneering scientists whose work offered validation and justification for his own indescribable experiences. His allusion, however, to someone 'who read widely and deeply in literature' (Baldwin 2000: 37) suggests that he did not see scientific knowledge and expertise as the only possible route in the acquisi-tion of the necessary reference points for the journey to self-surrender. The paradox of the 'very clearly, obviously present self', which can nonetheless surrender itself to a process, can be held in healthy tension, perhaps, through other modes of understanding. What seems for Rogers to be critical is the commitment of the therapist to the pursuit of learning and experience which can offer validation to subjective, personal knowledge and thus reinforce and enhance the ability to be fully present and to make possible the surrendering of self without fear of its permanent loss.

I have dwelt at some length on Rogers' interview with Michèle Baldwin, not only because it contains so much fascinating material about the state of his thinking in what was to prove the last year of his life but also because it bears all the marks of a man completely at peace with himself. The conversation is permeated by a sense of Rogers' inner freedom, which is the ultimate antidote to anxiety. A deep self-acceptance, in full consciousness of his flaws and vulnerability, is allied to a profound hope in the potential of persons and of humanity as a whole. There is a trust in the power of encounter to bring about transformation once energy can flow between persons without defensiveness. Above all, there is the calm, almost matter-of-fact, testimony of a man whose deep trust in his own experience has led him to the discovery of a greater reality of which he and others are an inseparable part. Content to some extent to live with a mystery and to savour such words as 'mystical', 'spiritual' and 'transcendent', Rogers is nonetheless nourished by the discoveries of scientific pioneers who feed his desire for meaning and empirical evidence.

As a young man, Rogers had struggled for many years with the idea of becoming a Christian minister. There were periods when he felt passionately close to God and when, released from the anxiety of having to submit to dogmatic beliefs, he was overwhelmed by feelings of universal compassion and the urge to communicate the 'good news'. And yet, at the age of 20 and still fresh from his formative trip to China as a member of a Christian expedition, he could write: 'Most of all perhaps, I have changed to the only logical viewpoint – that I want to know what is *true*, regardless of whether that leaves me a Christian or no' (Kirschenbaum 1979: 25).

Sixty-four years later in his interview with Baldwin, Rogers radiates the inner peace that comes from having pursued the truth to the best of his ability and from having remained faithful to his own experience. All the more remarkable, then, that the committed experientialist, empiricist and logical thinker should find himself entering a larger world where healing energies abound, where self-love engenders self-surrender and where hope into eternity seems an eminently rational attitude.

I am myself no scientist and cannot even claim to be a proper psychologist. If I have to resort to academic labels I must call myself a counsellor, a linguist, a student of literature, an educator and, with less confidence, an applied theologian of sorts. Perhaps such a list entitles me to claim the 'breadth of learning' which Rogers deems essential for a person-centred therapist. Be that as it may, I know that the self which I bring to my therapeutic work and to my everyday life is to a degree shaped and nourished by my 'learning' as much as by the experiences which life has brought me, some of them sought for and others unexpected and often unwelcome. I confess to a certain satisfaction that Rogers in this final interview should attach such importance to 'learning'. Often person-centred therapy is castigated as naïve, simplistic, unsophisticated, useful as a 'listening technique' for helpers and volunteers but not much use to 'real' psychotherapists. It is good that its originator should attach such importance to the 'learning' of its practitioners and to their familiarity with a wide range of human knowledge and wisdom. I am also aware, however, that Rogers, in seemingly paradoxical fashion, has commented only a few moments before in the interview that he knows some very good person-centred therapists who have had no training at all. He goes on to suggest that in small, remote villages, there will be those to whom others instinctively turn for help because they embody the characteristics of the person-centred therapist (Baldwin 2000: 37). There is, of course, no real contradiction here. The learning of which Rogers speaks is for him a part of the essential 'internalized landscape' which constitutes the self of the therapist. Its importance lies in the vital contribution it makes to the therapist's ability to be self-loving and to his or her courage in letting go of self in pursuit of the life-giving encounter.

The concept of 'learning' itself requires further illumination for it is difficult to believe that certain forms of 'learning' do much to encourage an
acceptance of self. On the contrary they can lead to a denigration of the
human person or even to an attitude where people become disposable in the
interests of some greater plan. It is certainly arguable, for example, that much
of the 'learning' induced by the media day in and day out fosters a contempt
for persons and depicts a world where hate, destructiveness and moral indifference reign supreme. In a technological age, too, some of the brightest
minds are devoted to the development of communication 'systems' whose
primary purpose is the maximizing of profits, the annihilation of competitors
and the promulgation of the faceless encounter as the preferred mode of
meeting. Such 'learning' leads not to self-acceptance and self-affirmation but
to the trivializing of the person in the interests of a brave new world, the
meaning of which is seldom questioned.

In the same way that learning can lead to contempt for the self, so, too, it
can foster a narrowness of vision which breeds prejudice and a fear of the
unknown. In an age of specialism there is no guarantee that even immersion
in higher education will provide the breadth of learning which Rogers
commends. On the contrary, there is every possibility that the entrapment
within a narrow field of knowledge and expertise will become increasingly
the norm. The hope that the internet will somehow encourage access to a
worldwide bank of knowledge and learning which will counteract such
cramping specialism is, I believe, a wistful fantasy. More likely is the
buttressing and reinforcement of specialized knowledge, the spread of
spurious data and weariness at information overload. Learning which impairs
the ability to cultivate a broad vision makes for fearful therapists, and it is in
this context that Rogers' reservations about the study of psychology become
so poignant.

The self-loving person does not go in fear of himself or herself; the person
with a breadth of learning is less likely to be scared of the unknown or of the
dangers of exploration. For Rogers, as for all person-centred therapists, every
meeting whether with a client or with anyone else was a potential journey
into the unknown. Psychology – like every stripling discipline – is keen to
assert its right over the terrain it considers its own. Such an aspiration easily
leads to false claims about the nature of human beings, their development,
their aberrations and their interactions. It was precisely this blinkered
approach, based upon an inflated view of psychology's claim to truth, which
made Rogers so apprehensive. For him, the human being was an awesome
creation, and his or her potential for self-understanding and self-transcendence through fearless relationship almost unimaginable. A person with
breadth of learning could rejoice in such evolutionary potential whereas the
psychologist, without the benefit of other more expansive disciplines, might

well disguise his or her fear of the unknown behind a façade of feigned omniscience. It is somewhat ironical that the man who in his youth had forsaken the study of theology and his apparent vocation to Christian ministry in order to embrace psychology should at the end of his life display such ambivalence towards the discipline to which he had devoted the best part of his career. Even more striking is his admission – again in the interview with Michèle Baldwin – that he was 'too religious to be religious' (Baldwin 2000: 35).

As I reflect upon my own career I observe some parallels with Rogers' experience but also some striking differences. I, too, changed tracks as a young man. Throughout my time as a student I had set my sights on becoming a teacher of language and literature but, unlike Rogers, I actually saw it through and entered my chosen profession. What is more, I had no reason to regret the decision: I enjoyed teaching and believed myself successful at it. The move into counselling was prompted by the discovery that many of my adolescent pupils were suffering abominably and that I seemed to have some ability to respond helpfully to their plight. I have no idea whether, for Rogers, the leaving of his theological studies and the abandonment of his Christian vocation was a source of grief, although what he has had to say about it suggests rather that it was a matter for relief and liberation. For myself, I know that leaving the classroom and the teaching of literature almost broke my heart. It seemed at the time that I was pursuing another path not because I truly wanted to but because I had no option. If this was a call it was one to which I responded with a heavy heart, while screaming inside at the unfairness of it all.

Embarking on the study of developmental and counselling psychology – albeit mostly in the client-centred tradition – also presented its difficulties. I have written elsewhere about my excitement and delight at the discovery of Carl Rogers' writings and their congeniality to me (Thorne 1989: 58–59), but in other ways the new discipline to which I was being subjected hit up against some profound resistance. There were times when I was appalled at what seemed to me a sadly limited view of the human being and of the inner world of men and women. In a determinedly conscious fashion, I resolved not to be hoodwinked (as I saw it) by an unbalanced perception of reality. Instead, I vowed to hold on to the knowledge which I already possessed as a result both of many years immersion in some of the finest literature that Europe has produced and also of my commitment to the Christian religion since boyhood. These two streams of knowledge and experience had contributed richly to my 'inner landscape' and were an integral part of the person I had become. Indeed, had that not been the case, I knew full well that I should never have taken the decision (to most of my friends bizarre and misguided) to abandon a profession I loved so dearly in order to embark on a problematical training for an, at that time, unknown and unregarded role which to the outside observer who was interested enough to enquire seemed a strange mix of social work and mental health education.

I often wonder what would have happened to me if during my counsellor training I had submitted to a kind of psychological brainwashing which was inherent not, I am sure, in the minds of most of my tutors but in some of the basic assumptions of the psychological material which I was required to study. The very style of some of those laborious treatises (analytical, behaviourist, statistical, experimental) gave the game away. They betrayed a lack of aesthetic sensibility, an apparent blindness to the truth of beauty as opposed to the ponderous evidence of so-called facts, and what seemed a wilful ignorance of or a scarcely veiled hostility to the claims of revealed religion.

Of one thing I am now certain: if I had not held on to the reference points which were already mine before I entered on my training and career as a person-centred therapist I should long since have given up on the task of being 'very clearly and obviously present' in my therapeutic relationships, or in any other relationship for that matter. Without the wider context provided by my 'breadth of learning' I am sure that, given the possibility of a transformational encounter, I would settle for a quiet life not out of laziness but out of fear. Rogers, it would seem, had the capacity to trust his personal experience with such pertinacity that he broke through to an apprehension of a spiritual domain which was then corroborated or at least supported by the discoveries of pioneering and controversial scientists. It is worth pondering, however, whether, unbeknown to him, his immense courage in relating was all along sustained by the breadth of learning and experience which he had already acquired before he embarked upon the study of psychology. I find it difficult to believe that the passionate Rogers of the early years – passion for God, passion for the world, passion for his sweetheart, Helen – was not still nourishing the eminent psychologist and psychotherapist of the mature years. The apparent reluctance on his part even to engage in discussion about religion during most of his professional career tends to confirm my hunch that the hidden and denied stream of spiritual awareness was powerfully operative throughout his life, emboldening his trust in his own experience and waiting for the comparative safety of old age before emerging once more into full consciousness. Perhaps much the same could be said of his passionate self as a sexual and sensual being which at the end of his life and after Helen's death found expression in a number of intense relationships with other women. Whatever the truth as far as Rogers is concerned, I know that, for myself, the fleeting and intermittent capacity I have for entering into relationships where spirit touches spirit and where 'something larger' is experienced partly owes its existence to the 'breadth of learning' afforded to me by my literary studies and by my attempt to embrace all that is life-affirming in the practice and understanding of the Christian religion. In more recent times this has meant for me the liberating experience of breathing the intoxicating air of mystical theology and discovering there the quintessence of a spiritual revelation which endows humanity with the glorious potential for divinization. For Rogers, pioneering scientists of the twentieth century brought him the assurance that to surrender himself in relationship was the ultimate and triumphant risk of being human; for me, my fellow citizen, the fourteenth-century mystical writer, Julian of Norwich, assures me that I am not mad to believe, in the words of Saint Athanasius, that 'God became man so that we might become God'. Perhaps, Rogers and I between us provide a glimpse of that 'breadth of learning and experience' which can make it possible for the person-centred therapist to invest his or her total self in relationship, conscious, paradoxically, of clear reference points in an unknown and mysterious land.

CHAPTER 8

Intimacy and sexuality

Before I begin, I know that this chapter will be the most difficult of all to write. In many ways, I would prefer not to embark upon it for it promises to make the heaviest demands on my capacity to express the inexpressible and is likely to render me vulnerable and open both to attack and to misunderstanding. Intimacy and sexuality can, of course, be discussed in an impersonal and coolly clinical way, but such a treatment would scarcely convey the level of passion, both personal and professional, which the two words engender for me. I am conscious of the seemingly outrageous claims that I have already made for person-centred therapy in previous chapters, but recognize that it is somehow easier to explore, for example, the wider bounds of science and religion than it is to enter the mysterious terrain of human relating at its most ecstatic and most agonizing. Not to attempt such a task, however, would be to lack the courage to explore the encounter which is at the heart of much therapy and which, in the person-centred tradition, constitutes the way of transformation. It is my conviction that the capacity to move into intimacy with the fearlessness which comes from the full integration of body, mind and spirit must be the person-centred therapist's supreme aspiration. Without such a capacity, the therapist can assuredly do good work but he or she will never be the agent of healing let alone the initiator of the mystical awareness which can bring about transformation.

Such an aspiration is, I would suggest, particularly foolhardy at the present time given the almost nightmarish dilemma in which the helping professions currently find themselves in terms of the relationships they can safely offer their clients. As our culture progressively reveals itself as abusive and emotionally punitive, the fear mounts in the helping professional of being accused himself or herself of abusive behaviour and of being the subject of vindictive litigation. Abused people desperately require the corrective experience of an affirming, deeply committed, non-abusive relationship in which they can find healing and discover hope for living. So profound is the woundedness in some cases, however, that the offering of such a relationship may well uncover an ocean of pain or provoke in the client a fear of seduction. The therapist who is prepared to accompany such pain or fear and even to face the possibility of being falsely accused will need exceptional courage and absolute trust in his or her own integrity. It is to the cost of such preparedness which this chapter must inevitably point.

Our society as a whole is failing lamentably to come to terms with sexuality. This should, perhaps, come as no surprise given the confusing shifts in attitude and behaviour of the last few decades of the twentieth century. It is a context, however, which profoundly affects the life of every individual no matter how varied the personal life experience may be. For the young person brought up in a secure and loving family environment as for the abused child of a dysfunctional household, the societal turbulence in matters of sexual behaviour and morality casts an unavoidable shadow. The contradictory messages which are now an everyday part of our social landscape have become so much taken for granted that I often wonder if their inherent and contradictory craziness has somehow become obscured from the majority. Not that the arena of sexuality is unique in this respect. The same craziness is to be observed in attitudes towards the ecological peril which our planet clearly faces. It takes one second's thought, for example, to perceive that the halting of global warming and the production of ever more motor cars are incompatible activities, and yet the latter continues unabated. In the same way it is self-evident that a culture which encourages undirected sexual arousal though its advertising industry and through its mass media cannot realistically expect to see the elimination of emotional and sexual abuse. These two are also incompatible and yet the former, with the advent of the internet, is escalating rather than diminishing. This endemic craziness, which can be seen in other spheres too, suggests an alarming split in the corporate consciousness, and there is no arena in which the consequences for individual wellbeing are potentially more dire than that of human sexuality. A powerful vignette comes to mind which illustrates only too clearly the unspeakable mess in which we have landed ourselves as a society.

A young acquaintance of mine, a talented woman, has recently entered the teaching profession. She is a committed and enthusiastic person who discovered her vocation when still in her early teens. In recent years, with the progressive demoralization of the teaching profession in Britain, many of her friends and even her parents have questioned the wisdom of her choice of career. Some of them have gone so far as to suggest that a person of her intelligence and personality should be seeking openings in the more prestigious areas of the commercial world. But Charlotte has not been deterred by these pressures and is now teaching in a large comprehensive school in the Midlands. In recent weeks, her life has been made a misery by a situation for which nothing during her training has remotely prepared her. She is a teacher of French, and motivating some of her pupils whose parents are unemployed and have never left the area where they were born is itself a mammoth task. They have no interest in French, can never imagine themselves going to France and see no point whatever in stretching their minds and imaginations to grapple with a subject which is utterly alien to them. Charlotte, however, does not give up easily. She has devised a number of dramatic role-plays in simple French where she takes a central part and hopes gently to encourage her disenchanted adolescent pupils to participate. The effect of this imaginative strategy has been electrifying but not in a way which Charlotte had even in her worst moments envisaged. It has unleashed in a small group of thirteen-year-old boys a torrent of sexually abusive remarks and behaviours. Charlotte has been called unspeakable names, accused of being a seductress and on one occasion publicly humiliated as she stood at a bus-stop near her home. Things came to a head when she was confronted at the end of a lesson by three highly disturbed boys who pressed her against the wall, fondled her and ran off laughing and jeering.

In the midst of this nightmare Charlotte has felt almost completely impotent. She has been unable to respond compassionately to the boys for fear of attracting more sexual innuendo; she has been fearful of responding robustly to their behaviour in case this should escalate their aggression; she has been terrified of touching them physically in case these young sexual abusers accused her, with sophisticated malice, of abusing them. Perhaps most distressing of all was her meeting with her headteacher, from whom she sought guidance and support. He told her in no uncertain terms that she was a fool to experiment with such 'progressive' methods of teaching and should change at once to more 'conventional' ways of instruction. She was made to feel that the sexual abuse and violation which she had experienced were her own fault and that he would be reluctant to defend her if the boys or their parents were to lodge complaints – however malevolently fabricated – against her.

This is to reveal the craziness of the corporate split consciousness in particularly florid form. Teachers, it would seem, are meant to tolerate even the most personally traumatic examples of the sexual confusion of a violent society and to accept that they are powerless to defend themselves or to retaliate for fear of being accused of the very abuse to which they have been subjected. In such a terrifyingly bizarre situation it seems unlikely that Charlotte and many other gifted and compassionate teachers will remain long in the profession. Indeed, to do so would be to put seriously at risk the preservation of a healthy and joyous sense of their own sexual identity. This, then, is the nature of the society in which a person-centred therapist aspires to offer his or her clients a relationship whose depth of intimacy promises healing and even transformation. It is clearly an aspiration fraught with no little danger.

For therapists from most other orientations the person-centred aim of being fully present to the client may seem a strange notion. To be attentive, alert, even openly caring and concerned, may be valued and commended. The conscientious cognitive behaviourist or analytical practitioner might well subscribe without difficulty to such humane objectives. Being fully present to another person is, however, of a different existential order, and takes the person-centred therapist into the hazardous terrain which inevitably opens up once there is a commitment to being congruent and resolutely faithful to the flow of experience. There is no better way of illustrating the potential nature of such terrain and of the challenges involved for the therapist than to plunge into the midst of a therapeutic process – only partly fictional and authentically illuminated by experience – and to track not only the dialogue between therapist and client but also something of the struggles within the therapist's mind, body and spirit. Reference to all three sources of energy is of central significance to the understanding of a process which is infinitely complex and of which the actual words spoken and the visible non-verbal behaviour are often but the tip of an ice-berg. What is more, in what follows, the various movements within the *client's* mind, body and spirit are only occasionally glimpsed and can only be intermittently understood in the light of subsequent developments. The therapist, for his or her part, is committed to being as present as possible in the relationship and cannot know, although he or she may well suspect, how present or absent the client is able or choosing to be. Repeated experience tells me, however, that the more I am able to be wholly involved in the relationship, the more likelihood there is that a meeting will take place which will prove healing for the client and from which I, too, may well emerge changed and more able to access the fullness of my own being.

The client is a young woman in her early 30s and I am her therapist. This is the third time we have met and already I know there is a strong bond between us. She has chosen to see me because she has heard of me from others and has read some of the things I have written, although I do not know exactly what and, despite my curiosity, I have not enquired. Such clients usually make me feel both flattered and apprehensive. I am glad that they have concluded that I may be capable of responding helpfully to them and yet at the same time I am fearful that I may not come up to expectations. These are tricky feelings and I have come to recognize how treacherous they can be. If I am not careful I shall fall into the trap of trying to be the 'great man', or, worse, I shall seek to please my client so that he or she will not feel let down and will experience my caring which, however genuine, will then be subtly or even grossly exaggerated.

As soon as I met Emma in the waiting room before our first session I knew we were likely to bond quickly. Not only was I aware as a result of an initial telephone contact that she had specifically chosen me and knew something of my work but her appearance was immediately energizing. I suppose there are therapists whose 'professionalism' determines that, for them, a client is a client is a client. I am not one of them and I know that I would not wish to be. For me, my professionalism requires that I do not deny but rather that I embrace my own personhood and celebrate the uniqueness of each client who crosses my threshold.

Why, then, was Emma's appearance for me in the waiting room 'energizing'? In some ways, the answer to that question will remain forever mysterious. In itself this is important for it introduces from the outset an element of the unknown which, for me, induces an attitude of excitement. In some ways, I suppose, all my clients have the capacity to provide this motivating excitement on first encounter, but, undeniably, some do it more than others. Emma undoubtedly scored highly on the excitement inducing scale. However unfathomable in its totality her energizing quality might have been, certain elements were very clear to me. I saw at once that Emma was young – at least in the eyes of a 60-year-old – and that she was, again in my eyes, an attractive woman. Her face had about it the somewhat ethereal quality of a pre-Raphaelite painting and her eyes were sad but nonetheless full of life. She was elegantly but not ostentatiously dressed and immediately she stood to greet me it was evident that she was beautifully proportioned. I was aware that I was in the presence of someone who in most social situations would have attracted more than the occasional sidelong glance of admiration.

All these impressions were registered in the first few seconds of meeting Emma in the waiting room. As I ushered her into my consulting room for the first time I knew that I was about to begin a relationship with a young woman for whom I already felt great warmth. What is more I knew that she was already drawn to me through my writings and reputation. The atmosphere in the room as we sat down together on either side of my coffee table was vibrant with energy. It is perhaps worth remarking that there are few other situations invented by human beings where an ageing 60-year-old man can sit down in the same room with an attractive 30-year-old woman and, without fear of interruption, be the recipient of her most private thoughts and feelings and the witness of her anguish and her yearning. The uncommon nature of this situation and the awesome quality of its implications need, I believe, to be stated and pondered. Certainly they should not be avoided or, worse still, dismissed as irrelevant to the conduct of a transaction between a professional and a client. For the person-centred therapist who acknowledges and even emphasizes that it is the quality of the relationship which will determine the outcome of the therapeutic enterprise, such avoidance or dismissal is not possible without courting complete hypocrisy and a total lack of integrity.

Although we are principally concerned here with the third session of Emma's therapeutic journey, I want to say a little more about the opening minutes of our relationship, not only because the beginning often determines much that follows but also because it illustrates in a particularly powerful way the inner world of a person-centred therapist. As I sat down with Emma and invited her to begin wherever she wanted, I was acutely aware of the multiplicity of thoughts and feelings flowing through me. To encourage and to attend to such awareness is an essential part of my professional responsibility as a person-centred therapist, as is the equally demanding task of deciding if and how to deploy such awareness in the interests of the client and of our relationship. At the risk of boring the reader with a turbulent cascade of apparently unrelated responses and reactions, I could cite the following:

I am flattered – honoured even – that this woman has chosen me.
I am acutely anxious that I shall let her down.
I am moved, almost to tears, by her sad but intensely vital eyes.
I feel an almost uncontainable warmth towards her.
She reminds me of a stained glass window.
It was Pope Gregory who said not Angles but Angels.
I am a fool whose fantasies could land him in deep trouble.
I wonder if her father is still alive.
Shall I be able to hold her? My God, in what sense do I mean that question?
I am Brian Thorne, a respected professor with a devoted wife and three
  grown-up children.
I would love to be an agent for good in her life.
If I don't watch it I shall be unable to listen to what she says.

In the event, two things occurred as a result of my staying with my kaleidoscope of thoughts, feelings and impressions and of forcing myself to discriminate between them. I was, in fact, able to give myself entirely to being alongside her inner world as, painfully, she gave me access to it and I gave expression, before we ended our first session, to certain things about myself. I told her that I was both glad and worried that she had sought me out and I acknowledged my fear of letting her down. I also told her that although I had no idea at this stage whether I could be of real help to her I felt warmly disposed towards her and had done so from the first moment of our encounter. My decision to offer her these glimpses of my own inner processes was not taken without considerable reflection. I concluded that to withhold such information would be to deny to her strong and persistent elements of my own experiencing to which her own openness with me somehow entitled her. She was beginning to trust me. I, in turn, wished to reciprocate that trust not in a way that would burden her with my concerns but so that she might sense my willingness to invest myself in the relationship – not as some kind of neutral expert, but as someone with his own inner world of thoughts and feelings who felt well disposed towards her.

When she left at the end of the first session Emma paused momentarily at the door of the building as I showed her out. To my astonishment there were tears in her eyes which she made no attempt to conceal. 'Thank you', she said, 'I think I shall be able to stay alive now.' And she was gone before I could reply.

Reflecting with my supervisor later in the week I had to acknowledge that I was well and truly hooked. Even talking about Emma made me tingle. I had seldom experienced such an overpowering desire for another's wellbeing and there could be no doubt that there was a strong sexual element in the warmth of my feeling for her. At least, that was how I interpreted it to myself for I still had a clear memory of her physical beauty and I could even, at times, recall the faint smell of the discreet perfume she was wearing. But, as far as I could tell, I had no desire to relate to her sexually: on the contrary, the idea was abhorrent to me and I concluded with relief that however lovingly disposed I was towards her I was not in love with her. Eros, it would seem, whatever part he was playing, was not in dangerous mood.

The second session threw me back into confusion for Emma took up where she had left off. Within minutes she was weeping profusely as she plunged into the account of her father's death when she was 14 and of the subsequent horror of her mother's remarriage, her own abandonment and the years of desolation and promiscuity which began at university and had finally ended in a psychiatric hospital after a nearly fatal overdose. She was now in a desperately unhappy marriage where she was made to feel worthless and she had been on the verge of attempting suicide once more when she had come for her first appointment the previous week. As I accompanied her through this painful narrative I was aware of an extraordinary vibrancy within myself which seemed to have the effect of endowing my empathic responses to Emma with an almost uncanny accuracy. Her distress gradually subsided and she seemed almost to be asleep as she allowed herself to drift into silence and what seemed a kind of serenity. For my part, I was anything but serene. I experienced an almost overwhelming desire to take her in my arms and to assure her than she was safe and that, despite the apparent evidence of her life so far, all could and would be well. I did neither of these things but nor did I try to push the feelings away. Instead I allowed myself to be full of the desire to protect her from harm and to find in myself the place where there is no anxiety. And I continued to regard her.

This word, regard, has come to have profound significance for me over the years. It has, of course, a double meaning which is the more apparent when I work in France where the word 'regarder' is the everyday word for 'to look at'. The other meaning is to esteem or to value, and when I speak of 'regarding' Emma I collate both these meanings to signify a dual activity of both the eyes and the heart. Certainly I looked at her in the sense that I held her in my gaze, but within my own being I nourished a sense of her infinite worth and of wonder at the potential fullness of her being. It is, I suppose, my hope that in some way a person who is thus 'regarded' experiences both my complete acceptance of their present state of being and my unshakeable faith in the process of their becoming. I know that at least in some cases such a hope has not been based on complete illusion for there are those – both former clients and trainees – who have told me that my confidence in them, long before they could experience it for themselves, has enabled them to find the courage to pursue their own path through life. What characterized my 'regard' for Emma in this second session, however, was the accompanying experience of vibrant energy surging through me which warmed my heart and sent currents through the whole of my body. Once again, I find it difficult to describe this as anything other than powerful sexual energy which was in no way trapped in the genitals but irradiated my whole being. Such energy has about it a force which engenders delight in the being and presence of the other irrespective of their current psychological state. Emma was clearly in deep distress but the energy which I experienced seemed enhanced rather than impeded by this fact. The session ended with a quiet acknowledgement on both our parts that we had moved through a storm and that far from being destroyed we were more closely bonded and had glimpsed a hope which lies beyond despair. Emma's final comment before she left was revealing: 'I'm amazed', she said, 'I feel so alive.' And before I could respond she suddenly hugged me and kissed me on the cheek.

I was left with feelings of delight and of alarm. I was delighted to be so apparently valued by a woman for whom I had such strong feelings of warmth and regard and, at the same time, I was alarmed that I had perhaps unwittingly triggered in her feelings of such passionate intensity that we would be in danger of drowning together. I know only too well that accurate empathy combined with a tender responsiveness can be a seductive brew and I was permeated by anxiety that in staying close to my own feelings and allowing them to persist I had inadvertently exercised a powerfully seductive influence on Emma. A more sinister thought was that I had abused my power in the mistaken belief that I desired only Emma's wellbeing and healing. This tortuous self-questioning was still with me when Emma appeared for her third session.

Immediately she sat down opposite me the questioning ceased. Once more I was permeated by feelings of overwhelming tenderness at her vulner-ability and a deep desire to be as fully present to her as I could be. Intimacy at the profoundest level is only possible, I believe, with someone who is willing to be present – body, mind and spirit – to the other, and I vowed to offer Emma the possibility of such intimacy if she wanted it. In that moment I knew I did not desire her, I was not in love with her, I did not wish to exercise power over her. I wanted her to know that she was worthy of my embodied self in all its complexity and that such embodiment must include, and even be permeated by, the sexual energy which nourishes my own vitality and creativity. What is more, I knew in that moment that the energy flowing through me was greater than I and that I was familiar with it in other settings, not least in those ecstatic experiences which have sometimes come to me unannounced on the hills of North Wales or in front of the Blessed Sacrament in cool Italian churches.

Emma sat silently for a while and I did not break the silence. It was some three minutes before she began:

E   Do you mind if I ask you something?
B   No, please do.
E   Do you think about me sometimes – outside these sessions, I mean?
B   Yes, sometimes I do that quite deliberately, but I sense that at some level you are seldom far from my consciousness. This matters to you, doesn't it? (I was surprised at the ease with which I found myself responding to her: somewhere at the back of my mind there was a fleeting fear that I could be walking into a trap but the responsibility of being honest seemed paramount.)
E   I find that amazing. Were you thinking about me last night about half past seven or so?
B   Yes. I was actually in church then and had you particularly in my thoughts. (I seldom tell my clients that I pray for them and would not dream of introducing my Christian beliefs or practices into a therapeutic relationship without invitation. My response to Emma on this occasion came from a powerful desire to be utterly truthful with her.)
E   (fighting back tears without much success) You love me, don't you? (These words were spoken in little more than a whisper and with an intonation of incredulity.)
B   Yes, I do – that is if love is measured by the depth of desire for someone's good. I so much long for your wellbeing and happiness that there are moments when I think I shall burst. (I knew that in speaking these words I had laid all my cards on the table and I felt immensely vulnerable.)
E   I think I knew that but I couldn't really believe it. You're not *in* love with me, are you?
B   No, Emma, I'm not in love with you, but I do feel pretty passionate about you. (The silence which followed this last exchange seemed to go on for a

long time. Indeed, I have no idea how long it lasted because it seemed to be outside of time and space. When she next spoke Emma seemed to be returning from far away and yet to my eyes she was more sharply delineated, and it was as if I had known her since the beginning of time.)

E   I thought for a moment just now that you were my father. He never knew me as a woman. (This direct, almost guileless, statement suggested to me that Emma had journeyed a long way during our period of silent reverie and was daring to face once more the pain of the past. I was concerned, however, not to voice what could only be tentative hypotheses.)

B   For a moment you felt I was your father but remembered that he had never seen you as a woman.

E   In some ways you *are* very much as I remember him. He was a pretty passionate man and never left me in any doubt that he loved me and thought I was wonderful. It was quite embarrassing at times. (For a minute or two, as the silence descended once more, I felt within myself the agonizing sense of desolation and abandonment which must have been Emma's when, unexpectedly and without warning, her father had died in her early adolescence.)

B   He loved you very much and then he left you. (I was aware that I avoided the word 'died' with its sombre sense of finality.)

E   (Tears were now streaming down her face as if they would never cease and yet, strangely, her words were clear and strong.) Yes, but just now I found him again and he loved me just as much. (And, with those words, Emma left her chair and threw herself into my arms and continued to weep without restraint. I held her with all the tenderness I could muster. Amusingly, I became concerned that her copious tears might be doing my new corduroy jacket irreparable damage! It was, I think, about a quarter of an hour later before Emma let go of me and returned to her own chair.)

E   My God! I'm sorry – I must have ruined your jacket. I'll pay to have it dry-cleaned.

B   Holy water has very special properties. (And we both laughed – the laughter of innocent children who, for a space, have regained paradise.)

Emma's therapy lasted for over a year, during which she left her husband, began to relate to her mother again and took herself back to university to train as a teacher. My love for her did not abate and there were times when the initial surge of vibrant energy coursed through my veins again as she struggled with some particularly painful aspect of her life. Our relationship and the intensity of much that happened between us gives rise to many questions about the person-centred approach to therapy and about the extraordinary terrain to which it sometimes gives access. These questions and the reflections which they engender are the subject of the next chapter.

CHAPTER 9

'Alive alive'

The explanation which follows of what was happening in the first three sessions with Emma may seem off the wall to many and will undoubtedly earn the scorn or even the professional condemnation of some. I offer it now as a prelude to a much fuller discussion of the implications for the life and work of a person-centred therapist when the approach is conceptualized as an essentially mystical response to human beings and their destiny.

Emma, it will be recalled, was on the verge of despair and self-destruction when she sought me out. She also knew something about me from my writings and from what others had told her. She came therefore in hope, which must not be confused with optimism. Hope can be entertained in the face of formidable odds, whereas optimism, which blindly persists despite all the evidence against it, smacks of self-deception or an obstinate evasion of the facts. Hope, I would suggest, exists outside or beyond the confines of rational or logical discourse: it is itself an attitude which, however faintly entertained, issues from a different apprehension of reality.

It so happened that Emma touched something in me which, from the outset, gave to our relationship a quality of exceptional intensity. Not to put too fine a point on it, the very sight of her triggered in me a vibrancy and a vitality which meant that I was immediately firing on all cylinders in her presence. Indeed, I was initially almost overwhelmed by my own energy and feared that I might be engulfed in a maelstrom over which I would have little control. It is not irrelevant that in my eyes Emma was beautiful. Beauty can, of course, lead to perdition as many a luckless lover has discovered, but it can also engender intimations of truth and of goodness. I would suggest that, for me, Emma's beauty awakened precisely my own yearning for truth and goodness and that her arrival confronted me with a moral imperative to give of my very best at every level. But there was more to it than that. I knew before I met her that Emma valued me. She had read some of my writings and had been attracted by them. She had also had a 'good report' of me from others. The aliveness in her sad eyes which shone out at me in the first seconds of our meeting conferred worth on me whatever ambivalent feelings I might have had at being the recipient of her expectations. This beautiful woman, then, valued me, enabled me to feel fully alive and awakened in me a passionate yearning for goodness and truth. She left me in no doubt, too, that however much I might rejoice in my own autonomy and independence, I am essentially a relational being, made not for self-sufficiency but for communion.

This recognition of ultimate interdependence as the cornerstone of identity also served me well in my initial meetings with Emma. I knew that alone I could do nothing for her. Everything would depend on how she and I could be together, how we could collaborate (literally work together) in the exploration of her life and its difficulties and challenges. She needed me but I needed her if we were to accompany each other in this hazardous journey. As a person-centred therapist I believe that the resources are in the client and are waiting to be discovered if only I can offer a relationship of unconditional affirmation characterized by deep and compassionate empathy. But I also know that even this – exceptional and life-saving as it can be – will be less efficacious than a relationship where, in addition, I can dare to be fully present and to put my whole being at the service of my client when this is needful for his or her growth and healing. My client is helped by knowing that I am not a superior being but human too, with my fears and vulnerabilities and that, despite them, I am prepared to take the risk of being in relationship. I know that, for me, the ultimate test of the level of collaboration between my client and me in a therapeutic relationship is whether I can trust my client as much as I hope he or she will trust me. When that occurs I am free to be fully me, not with the purpose of having my own needs met but so that I am released to be a channel for the healing energy by which I believe we are constantly surrounded.

I have no doubt that in those first exhilarating sessions with Emma I was enabled to be such a channel. In some ways if that had not been the case I sense I could have foundered on the rocks of an unbridled eroticism or an undisciplined sexuality. As it was, I did my best to open myself to the healing and transformational energies on whose aid I know I must ultimately rely. When Emma asked me in the third session whether I had been thinking about her at 7.30 on Wednesday evening I could not have known, as she told me later, that at that time precisely her husband was threatening to disfigure her with a broken bottle. What I did know, however, was that I desired the whole company of Heaven to watch over her as I prayed passionately for her in the Shrine of Julian of Norwich – a place hallowed for me by the knowledge that 600 years previously my fellow citizen, the great medieval mystic, was exercising her vocation as she counselled through the window of her anchoress's cell (Thorne 1999).

Although at the time I did not know which of my writings Emma had read it was clearly possible that she was already aware of my spiritual convictions and religious affiliations. At the very least there was a likelihood that she knew that I inhabited a world which was not confined to a purely psychological understanding of reality. Be that as it may, my response to her direct question about my attentiveness to her outside the therapeutic hour served to confirm both my level of commitment to her and the expansiveness of the psychic terrain which I inhabit. Given all this, I would suggest that it was perhaps not surprising that my capacity to be fully present to her engendered an intensity of relating which enabled her, too, to move beyond the immediate confines of our physical environment and the dynamics of our relationship. It would seem that she entered the 'something larger' to which such communion gives access and found there the father whom she had lost and his internalized love for her which had always been present but had for so long eluded her awareness. If this explanation of the process in which we were involved comes anywhere near the truth, its implications are, of course, enormous. In brief, I am suggesting that for a whole host of reasons I was able to be fully present to Emma with the totality of my being and that her response to me resulted in both of us being transported to a level of being where resources were available to us which profoundly affected the process of her therapeutic journey. A further implication is that once we had accessed such a level of being or, to use the expression employed by Rogers, we had moved to an 'altered state of consciousness', the level of trust between us increased immeasurably. We were both released, it seemed, to be fully alive with each other and to trust each other's essential goodness.

Rogers himself was always cautious about using the word 'good'. So great was his awareness of the damage done to many people by being labelled 'bad' or 'evil' that he wished to avoid such polarized language altogether. He preferred to speak of the essential core of the human being as being 'forward-moving' but he certainly regarded this core as trustworthy. It was, I believe, the experience of a mutual trustworthiness that enabled Emma and me to be both fearless in our intimacy and also at home in a world infinitely more resourceful than that to which our separate identities would have given access without the added gift of such profound mutuality.

It would be perhaps easy to dismiss my experience with Emma – whatever judgement is passed upon it, favourable or unfavourable – as altogether exceptional and of little general usefulness in considering the day-to-day work of a person-centred therapist. A cynical commentator might well observe that few clients are likely to elicit such immediate and highly charged responsiveness and that few therapists have written so openly about themselves as I have done with the result that Emma knew me in some important way before she crossed the threshold of my consulting room. Or to put it more bluntly: not many clients trigger such powerful energy in their therapists, nor do they bring with them a knowledge of and at least provisional validation of the person whose help they are seeking. And, anyway, it could be argued that I was saved from folly or worse by the fortuitous convergence of my sexual and my spiritual energy without which the process might have turned out very differently.

Despite all this, my intention in what follows is to entertain the hypothesis that my relationship with Emma, far from being an exceptional and therefore irrelevant example of a therapeutic process, provides, in fact, a telling insight into the essential heart of person-centred therapy and its transformational power. Such a hypothesis in no way denies the utter uniqueness of my relationship with Emma, for it is a basic assumption of person-centred therapy, as Peggy Natiello has expressed it recently in her beautiful book *The Person-Centred Approach: A Passionate Presence*, that 'the relationship is unique in each situation, and grows out of the unanticipated and unrehearsed interactions between two particular people' (Natiello 2001: 26).

Although it is in some ways embarrassing and runs the unenviable risk of being thought presumptuous or arrogant, I have no option but to begin with myself. Again, as Peggy Natiello has succinctly and disarmingly put it, any discussion has to address questions about 'our ability to enter into an intimate, authentic, trustworthy relationship with another' (Natiello 2001: 25). Furthermore she sees the therapist's therapeutic relationships as being 'about *who we are* – the spiritual, emotional, attitudinal characteristics that we embody as persons, our ability to make a deep connection, to tolerate intimacy, and to offer a climate of safety' (Natiello 2001: 25). To do justice to such a radical and far-reaching statement would necessitate a full autobiographical study on my part and clearly this is neither possible nor desirable at this juncture. I shall confine myself to certain key issues which I perceive as relevant to my state of being and therefore to my preparedness for Emma's arrival in my life. I claim no particular merit for what follows. It is simply a factual record of what might well be termed 'relevant data'.

I have been a person-centred therapist for more than 30 years and married for longer than that. During those years I have known many forms of intimacy and have undertaken long and unpredictable journeys with members of my family, my clients, my friends and my colleagues. These journeys have provided me with some of the most exquisite and awesome experiences of my life: they have also, at times, taxed me to the limit of my resources and, on occasion, they have been the source of much pain and anxiety. It is also perhaps significant that I speak two foreign languages and that I have been privileged to enjoy from an early age a number of close relationships with persons of different cultures. I do not believe, however, that such experiences would have been possible for me if I had not embarked at a much earlier age on a spiritual journey, the immensity of which even now sometimes leaves me incredulous.

To say that I embarked upon that journey is perhaps not strictly accurate: it makes the whole process sound too purposeful and too conscious. As I reflect today on the key experiences of my childhood which profoundly affected the course of my life, it would be nearer the truth to say that they were *given* to me. I suppose I must in some way have been ready for them and, in that sense, I played my part, but the experiences of the reality of God and of my own belovedness in the scheme of things were not something which I consciously sought. They were a gift – unmerited and initially unconceptualized – which it took me many years to internalize. I was also to discover that they were by no means the experience of everyone. On the contrary, many people seemed to find it difficult, in fact impossible, to believe in God and most seemed to have little sense that they were of infinite worth and essentially lovable and desirable. It was not until 1962 that, in the writings of Julian of Norwich, I found a soul mate who expressed perfectly what I had always known: that if I – and Julian – were infinitely beloved by a God who was all love then this must be true of every human being. If she and I were the 'darlings' of God then it followed that everyone else was, too, whether they were conscious of this or not. This conviction was deeply rooted in me long before I began my training as a person-centred therapist in 1967. At the heart of the conviction was the understanding that my infinite belovedness – even when I behaved badly – was guaranteed by the fact that God had taken up residence in my humanity and that there was nothing I could do to dislodge him. As Julian assured me, there was a part of me that was inseparably linked to God and always would be and, this being the case, not to accept my own belovedness was somehow to accuse God of wasting his time on a useless object. Like Julian, I have always had difficulty with the concept of sin, but if, as she suggests, sin has no reality except in its outworkings, then there is plenty of evidence to suggest that the failure to acknowledge one's own worth and the many human attitudes and activities which prompt and reinforce such a universal failure are largely responsible for the world's despair and misery.

Self-acceptance is a wonderful thing but to experience oneself as infinitely lovable and desirable goes a stage further. This, I would suggest, is the passionate self-love which has absolutely nothing to do with selfishness and everything to do with self-forgetfulness. Self-love of this order, because it means freedom from self-preoccupation, gives access to unbounded energy which is then available for living in the moment without anxiety. As I attempt now to relate the fruits of my spiritual journey to my state of being when I first encountered Emma, I conclude that everything that had preceded our meeting and everything about her enabled me to be fully present and to be so aware both of my own essential belovedness and of hers that I was able to give myself to the energy flowing through me without fear of doing harm.

I have come to see this sense of being infinitely beloved as the key to the integration of sexuality into one's total responsiveness to another person or, indeed, to the created order in general. Sexual energy can clearly be a formidable force, and its potential for destructiveness is inevitably heightened when it is fuelled by an overriding need to possess or to control. If I feel essentially unvalued or, worse, abandoned or rejected, my need for validation can be so great that only the possession of another person will provide the way out of my loneliness – or so I falsely believe. Again, if I feel powerless or, worse, humiliated and victimized, it may be that to seduce another person or, in the worse case, to perpetrate their emotional or physical violation will restore to me – or so I falsely believe – a sense of my own power and of my ability to control the lives of others. Sexual energy in these instances becomes a monstrous and unanchored force which perversely and destructively sets out to remedy a lack of self-love or personal power, but in the process not only does untold damage to others but also, in the long run, intensifies my own sense of personal worthlessness and impotence. It is against this background that the therapist must be sure of his or her own existential worth and freedom from power seeking if there is to be any likelihood of sexual energy informing and, indeed, irradiating the total response to a client in a way which can bring life and healing. For my own part, it is only when I experience a profound conviction of my belovedness, no matter what may happen to me, that I am able to let go of anxiety and fear and offer myself to another person in trustfulness that the process – whatever the difficulties – will work out well. Such a sense of belovedness, although enhanced and buttressed by the love and validation of other human beings, cannot, I believe, be securely founded on them alone. I know that I am only free to be fully myself – and that means with every part of my being – when I am utterly caught up in a stream of love which pours itself out unreservedly on the whole universe. What is more, when I am secure in such all-embracing love, not only do I have no desire to possess or exert power over another person but such a desire is abhorrent to me. It is as if my whole being undergoes a transformation and I become transparent, empathic, compassionate and yearn only that the other may become self-loving and fully alive. Miraculously, too – and I believe it is of the order of miracles – the whole universe seems ready to offer its resources to two human beings who, because they are fully alive in the moment, have been swept up into eternity. These last sentences can clearly be interpreted as an attempt to find words for the inexpressible by resorting to unashamedly mystical language. For me, however, they are but another way of conveying what Carl Rogers was seeking to express when he spoke of being fully present to another human being and of the entry into 'something larger' which could then occur. I have also suggested earlier that this measured and secular use of language in order to give access to what he nonetheless acknowledges as a 'spiritual', 'mystical' and 'transcendent' experience is perhaps predictable in someone who had spent most of his professional life in denial of an order of experiencing which as a young man he had enthusiastically embraced. This is not an attempt to reclaim Rogers for the Christian fold. It is, however, to suggest that at the deepest level, his earlier vocation to the Christian ministry and his subsequent career as a psychologist and psychotherapist were by no means as divorced as many have believed or as he himself seemed resolutely to maintain. I am reminded of our visit together to the Prado in Madrid on Easter Sunday 1978 and of Carl's encounter with a vast portrait of Saint Thomas, the doubting apostle. His comment, 'Ah, my patron Saint', seems to me, in retrospect, wholly characteristic of someone whose commitment to empirical evidence had in no way extinguished a preparedness to conceptualize the existence of a world beyond the confines of current empirical enquiry. Indeed, his even greater commitment to the validity of his own experience left him with no option but to maintain an openness of mind and heart (Thorne 1991: 128-29).

'Something larger' is a nebulous enough term and I can only surmise what it might have meant for Rogers when he first used it, let alone what it might have come to mean in the years following. For me, however, as I think of my work with Emma and of many clients before and since, there are some elements which serve as clear reference points in the vast immensity of the mystical universe. The first may sound strange 'as a clear reference point' for, in a sense, it is neither clear nor a 'point'. I refer simply to the existence of an invisible world which lies beyond the normal range of consciousness. Believing in the invisible world has never presented me with much difficulty. Indeed, not to believe in it would seem infinitely more difficult given the fact that such invisible forces as love, hate, joy, suspicion and fear, not to mention the elemental power of the wind, clearly have immense impact on human lives. Most of us, too, have the regular experience of walking into a room and being filled with alarm - or delight - although we see, hear or smell nothing particularly unusual. It is as if an invisible world breaks through into our consciousness and we are compelled to acknowledge its presence and its influence. Interestingly, too, two people can walk into the same room and only one may be assailed by the power of the invisible leaving the other mystified or even contemptuous of his or her companion's experience. The point I am making is this: the belief in the existence of an invisible world must, by definition, radically affect my response to everything. It does not imply a neglect, let alone a contempt for the visible world. On the contrary, the breathtaking discoveries of scientific enquiry in the last hundred years demonstrate that it is precisely a profound respect and curiosity about what is visible and available to the five senses that lead to the incontrovertible evidence of an invisible reality. In some cases, with the aid of technological inventiveness, what was formerly invisible is indeed rendered visible. We can, for example, now see, thanks to our microscopes and telescopes, what previous generations could only intuit or dream about. Nor is it perhaps irrelevant that those who first postulated the existence of such invisible worlds (now rendered visible) were often considered mad or, at best, wildly eccentric.

When I met Emma I believed in the existence of an invisible world and this, I suggest, gave to our encounter from the outset an infinitely greater context than that provided by the immediately obvious framework of an initial session between therapist and client. There was, to start with, the immensity of nearly one hundred years of the combined lived experience of two human beings. This in itself promised a resourcefulness of staggering proportions. If to this is added the vastness of a cosmic universe, the potential resourcefulness is beyond words. In brief, my belief in the invisible world – if truly embraced – engenders an attitude of deep trustfulness in the resources of my client, in my own resources and, most importantly, in the untold riches and wonders of the 'something larger' by which we are surrounded. Indeed, the absence of such an attitude would seriously call into question the validity of the belief or, at the very least, the genuineness of my profession of it.

To my belief in the existence of an invisible world must be added the accompanying conviction of the presence in that world of a whole host of benevolent forces. These range from my awareness of the love in which I am held by my family, my friends and many others whose lives I have touched in some way, to the protection of saints and angels and the whole company of Heaven. The nature of my religious experience makes it possible for me to postulate a divine activity of which I am an inseparable part. With this trust in such an activity comes an immediate awareness of a connectedness with such powerful forces for good that all straining and striving cease and I am able to be fully alive in the present moment. I sense that Carl Rogers was attempting to give expression to the same phenomena when he saw the actualizing tendency in human beings as being a part of the formative tendency which permeates the entire cosmos. Be that as it may, what I know is that in my time with Emma there were many occasions when, for me, a sense of our connectedness to each other and to all that is was so deeply pervasive that my words, behaviour and the whole flow of my inner experiencing were reflections of a total freedom from anxiety and of a willingness to participate fully in a process which we jointly permitted but did not seek to control.

A belief in the invisible world and in the benevolent forces by which it is permeated runs the risk of being caricatured as a pollyannish and naïve fantasy in the same way that Rogers' concept of human nature was, and is, seen by many as the wildly optimistic perception of someone who ignores half the evidence of the world about him. It can be justifiably argued that the existence of benevolent forces in no way rules out the existence of their malevolent counterparts and that both the human psyche and the history of humankind provide ample data to support this counterbalancing hypothesis. I would not wish to deny this, and Rogers, too, both in his response to Rollo May (cf. Thorne 1992: 80) and on other occasions, readily acknowledged, as we have seen, that the 'problem of evil' would not go away and that he was far from satisfied with his own reflections on the matter. It is, I believe, irrefutable that highly destructive forces can take up residence in me as in all human beings, and I have little difficulty in believing that they can be equally active in other dimensions of the invisible world. In centuries past, and for millions of people today, a belief in demonic powers was a fundamental part of their perception of reality and, although I find such a metaphor unhelpful, I would not wish to dismiss or to trivialize the phenomena it attempts to interpret. The question for me is not whether evil – or whatever other name we may wish to give it – exists. I am prepared to accept the hypothesis as an eminently reasonable attempt to make sense of the data in the same way that Julian could accept sin on the evidence of its outworkings. By far the more important question is how, given that destructive forces are rampant, can they be overcome. The claim I am making, which constitutes the main *raison d'être* for this book, is that person-centred therapy has at its core an answer to that question. Furthermore, the heightened intensity of a therapeutic relationship, such as the one I have attempted to describe with Emma, goes some way towards elucidating both why and how such an apparently outrageous and grandiose claim can find convincing support in experience. I will attempt now both to summarize the process of that relationship and to reiterate my contention that, far from being an exceptional and therefore irrelevant case, it serves to illuminate the essential heart of all person-centred therapeutic activity.

Emma made it easy for me to embody the core conditions. She had validated me before we ever met by deliberately choosing me as her therapist on the basis of what she already knew about me. She immediately triggered powerfully positive feelings in me by her physical beauty and by her open responsiveness. She motivated me to be as fully present to her as possible and to lay aside anxiety as I risked trusting myself, trusting her and trusting an unpredictable process. Offering her unconditional positive regard, entering empathically into her inner world and being powerfully in touch with the flow of my own experience were not difficult. Indeed, they seemed to me a wholly natural expression of living fully in the moment with a fellow human being with whom I felt an immediate and deep connection. From time to time, destructive shadows flickered into awareness. There were momentary longings to possess and to be possessed by so lovely and vulnerable a person and the transitory fear of being swept away by overpowering forces which would have no regard for her wellbeing. But they were only flickering shadows: they had no lasting power in the context of a relationship which gave access with remarkable swiftness to an 'altered state of consciousness' where healing energies abounded. Emma and I were released into an eternal present where we could be fully alive and, as a result, she moved away from the allurement of death and increasingly embraced life or, in the words of Goff Barrett-Lennard, she moved decisively from woundedness to hope (Barrett-Lennard 1998: 110). Her experience – and mine – of a process which can only be adequately described in mystical, spiritual terms triggered the delayed grief for her father, the end of her marriage, the healing of the relationship with her mother and the start of a new and satisfying career. To live fully in the present, it would seem, enables the past to be overcome and the future to be embraced. What is more, the commitment of the therapist to living out the core conditions not only ensures a freedom from anxiety but renders much more likely this very movement into the eternal present. The emphasis on the unconditional affirmation of the other also ensures that empathic under-standing is not employed manipulatively and that whatever dark forces are present in the flow of inner experience cannot achieve pre-eminence. To put it as succinctly as possible, the person-centred therapist who commits himself or herself to the living out of the core conditions is exercising the spiritual discipline which is the expression of a practical mysticism. The potential end result of such a discipline is the release of the divine energies which permeate the whole created order but which our customary anxieties and selfish preoc-cupations prevent us from acknowledging, let alone accessing.

It is my contention that this is the essential transcendent truth at the heart of person-centred therapy and that my relationship with Emma provided incontrovertible evidence of its power. The experience of being fully alive with another person is, I would suggest, more profound than being 'in love' although it engenders much of the same delight and vibrancy. The intima-tions of truth and beauty which Emma engendered for me are there in each and every client, however obscured or marred, and it is my task to be as fully alive in their presence as I was with her. If I truly believe in my own essential belovedness and if I believe that living out the core conditions with another person gives access to untold forces of healing then I have no need of an Emma to buttress my conviction. The depressed middle-aged man sitting in the waiting room for his first appointment is as much part of the divine inter-connectedness as she or I. My task is to be with him in such a way that he can come to recognize his own nature. If we can both be truly alive in the present moment, then the past will lose its stranglehold and the future will take care of itself.

Some years ago a remarkable woman applied to join the training course for person-centred therapists which I directed at that time in the University of East Anglia. She spoke to my colleague and me for over an hour on the telephone from Kigali, the capital city of Rwanda. This was shortly after the appalling period of genocide in that country where many thousands of Rwandans had been butchered by their own compatriots in bitter tribal conflict. She had lost her husband, her mother and father and many other friends and relatives in the massacres. Why, I asked at the end of our conversation, did she really wish to come all the way to Norwich in England to train as a person-centred therapist? I shall never forget her reply to that question. 'I have a dim hope,' she said, 'that you might be able to restore my faith in human nature.' Many months later she was sitting in the middle of a community meeting as a member of the training group to which she had contributed so much through her suffering but also, increasingly, through her radiant joy. The group was battling, as so often, with the daunting and frequently demoralizing questions which confront therapists in their seemingly hopeless tasks. This woman who had suffered unimaginable pain and witnessed horrific atrocities beyond the imagination of most of us began to speak with immense passion. I do not recall much of what she said on that occasion but the hope which she embodied was palpable and clearly had its source above and beyond the horror and despair which she had so recently experienced. She ended, however, with unforgettable words. 'It is no use being alive,' she said, 'we must be alive alive.' I have come to think that in those two words she perhaps summed up the whole matter. To be 'alive alive' is to risk being fully present to another in the conviction that we can trust the core of our own beings. We are members one of another and are made for communion, however unbridgeable the divisions may appear. I know, too, that for me this Rwandan survivor has become an inexhaustible source of inspiration and validation. Her experience had plunged her into the very jaws of hell as she found herself engulfed in one of the most obscene and horrific episodes of a century characterized by mass violence and barbarity. When she spoke to us on the phone from Kigali and told us that she glimpsed in the person-centred approach to therapy the faint possibility of having her hope in humanity restored, I was awestruck. When, later, it turned out that her intuition had not been misplaced and that she had indeed rediscovered hope for herself, her children and her country, I was forced to acknowledge that the age of miracles is not past and that to speak of person-centred therapy as a spiritual discipline and to regard its practitioners as practical mystics is not only defensible but wholly appropriate.

CHAPTER **10**

When the world stopped turning

In Chapter 7, I dwelt at some length on an interview which Carl Rogers gave during the last year of his life. I suggested that the skill of his interviewer, Michèle Baldwin, together with his own sense of fulfilment enabled Rogers on this occasion to be particularly expansive in his thinking and to give voice to previously unformulated hopes and perceptions. Not very long ago, I was fortunate enough to experience something of the same kind of liberating opportunity when I was interviewed by Alison Leonard, a writer and broad-caster, in connection with a book which has subsequently appeared under the title *Living in Godless Times* (Leonard 2001). An account of the inter-view constitutes pages 160–75 of Alison's book and, with her and the publisher's permission, it is included as an appendix to this present volume. The interview, because it followed a largely autobiographical thread, enabled me to make connections between the events in my life and my religious, spiritual and therapeutic experiences. In many ways it is a kind of 'apologia pro vita mea' and will, I hope, further illuminate some of the themes I have attempted to explore in previous chapters.

Re-reading Alison's account of our interview, however, shows me how precarious my vision is and how uncertain the path ahead. The interview ends on a note of waiting and there was, I know, for me at the time a sense of apprehension as well as of hope in the waiting. Certainly the interview gives only veiled indications of the despair and the anger which I often experience in the face of many trends in our contemporary culture and of the way in which these have also contaminated the world of counselling and psychotherapy. In the past 20 years the emphasis on efficiency, cost-effective-ness, accountability and driving up standards has resulted in a context where a view of the person has developed which leaves little room for the validation of personal uniqueness or the exercise of empathic compassion. Persons have become 'units of resource', the success of an enterprise is measured almost entirely in financial terms and a basic principle seems to be that nobody is trustworthy. Everyone must therefore be monitored and assessed

87

and the field is wide open for accusation and counter-accusation, for the attaching of blame and the spread of guilt and shame. The resort to litigation on the most trivial pretext is now commonplace, and there are even new and profitable organizations which aggressively encourage people to seek redress through the courts whether or not they really wish to do so (cf. Thorne 1997). The language which has developed alongside this descent into the gross reification and commercialization of most human relationships and activities tells its own story. It is a language devoid of soul which concerns itself with control, judgement and the primacy of economic criteria. A glossary of terms which would seek to do justice to this arid scenario would run to many pages and would include such currently fashionable favourites as the 'delivery of services' – as if education and health were commodities rather like groceries and not concerned with the most sensitive aspects of human development and wellbeing. It is depressing to contemplate, too, that there may no longer be satirists who would rejoice to parody an administration capable of generating within a stone's throw of each other (as the Labour government has done since 1997), a 'Delivery Unit', an 'Office of Public Sector Reform', a 'Performance and Innovation Unit' and a 'Forward Strategy Unit' – thus creating overlapping 'command and control' centres of astonishing complexity.

The confusing irony behind some of these politically inspired initiatives is that there is a declared and probably honest intent to create a more just society where human potential can flourish, equal opportunities become a reality and the 'good life' be accessible to all. The tragedy lies in the adoption of methodologies which pay scant regard to human vulnerability and in the largely unexpressed but clearly assumed belief that the 'good life' consists of material rewards and depends on economic superiority. It is as if an ideal world is postulated but that in the process the human beings who will inhabit it have been left out of account and the essential emptiness of the idealized vision itself cannot be questioned in the corridors of political power.

In the writing of a book there is always for me the conflict between wanting to draw on current experiences and events and the more ambitious desire to produce something which will have validity, if not for all time, at least for a decade or two. There are many instances in previous chapters where, hesitantly, I have allowed myself to adopt the style of a diarist. I have referred to my current preoccupations, to contemporary events in the world, even to my passing reflections as I sit in a train or in my university office. This uneasy tension has resulted, I know, in some obsessional repetition and may have made for difficulties for a reader who is not accustomed to moving between scholarly discourse and a personal journal. As I write today, however, this conflict reaches its climax, because there is no way in which I can pursue the thread of this final chapter without reference to the fact that our common experience of the world has profoundly changed since I began writing it.

On 11 September 2001 – only four days ago as I write – the United States of America suffered the most devastating and horrific terrorist attack in its history. The World Trade Center in New York lies in ruins, the Pentagon is partially destroyed and the number of innocent civilian victims is in the thousands and still rising. Among those killed are many British citizens. As yet, the enemy which has inflicted this terrible slaughter remains unknown, although the evidence points increasingly towards fanatical Arab Muslim groups whose hatred of America is so intense that self-immolation and the annihilation of thousands of human lives are the monstrous but grotesquely logical outcome. The world is in a state of appalled shock, and in the midst of unprecedented global mourning and a spontaneous outpouring of grief and support for America, there is a terrifying and eerie hiatus. The world is waiting in fear for what will happen next.

In a strange, and in some ways shameful, sense, the events of the past few days have made me feel less bizarre and less absurdly alarmist in what I have written in many of the preceding chapters. I have constantly alluded to the knife-edge on which I believe the human race to be poised and I have attempted to spell out the challenges which confront us as a species if we are to survive. It is not now possible, I believe, either to refute the essential validity of my analysis, or to deny the urgency of the task.

One extraordinary outcome of this week's catastrophe has been the apparently spontaneous unity of many of the world's nations in the corporate experience of silence. The worldwide observance of a three-minute period of silent reflection in honour of those who lost their lives seems to have engendered a sense of solidarity and interconnectedness which has transcended national boundaries, cultural differences and religious beliefs. The columnist Paul Vallély, who most frequently writes on religious and spiritual matters, reports this shared international silence in today's *Independent*. This unprecedented news item commands almost the entire front page of the newspaper – not the customary place, perhaps, for the reflections of a religious affairs correspondent – and concludes with four memorable sentences:

> For just three minutes yesterday the world stopped turning. Instead it stood still in a simple but tearful homage.
> And yet the result was not depressing. It was a moment of curious enrichment and inspiration.
>
> (Vallély 2001)

It is not, I believe, fanciful to see this astonishing corporate experience, shared by millions of people, as the powerful outcome of an immediate empathic responsiveness. The death and suffering of loved ones strikes deep into the consciousness of even the most unimaginative and insensitive person. So fundamental are the human emotions involved that empathy becomes easy and almost instinctive. So, too, does congruence for it is scarcely possible not to be aware of a deep internal sadness and grief which spring not only from sharing the pain of others but also from the re-triggering of one's own suffering and the fearful knowledge of humanity's common mortality. In the midst of such deep and shared emotions it also becomes natural and instinctive to respond openly and non-defensively to others so that in the grieving crowds around the world total strangers fell into each other's arms and offered comfort and support without inhibition and without reservation. The manifest, unashamed and mutual vulnerability released an energy which neither conditioning nor the fear of adverse judgement could impede. It would not, perhaps, be disrespectful to add to Paul Vallély's masterly report a final paragraph for person-centred readers:

> For three precious minutes millions of people throughout the world knew what it means to live the core conditions and to be fully present to each other. For a moment, too, they experienced a mystical and transcendent interconnectedness which spoke of a hope beyond despair.

What, however of the terrorists? They, too, are part of the human family although there are few apparently whose voices are currently raised to affirm their membership. Their deeds, it is implied, are so evil, so demonic, so utterly contemptible that they have forfeited the right to be called human. It would seem as if they must be the scapegoat to be expelled from the face of the earth so that the rest of the tribe can continue to exist. It has always been thus in the history of humankind as the philosopher/sociologist René Girard has repeatedly illustrated in books which, understandably perhaps, are too much for many of us to bear. It is always easier to have a scapegoat on whom blame can be heaped and condemnation pronounced than to look within to see if, just conceivably, some of the evil – however little – may be lodged there (Girard 1996).

Should the terrorists eventually be firmly identified – not only those who perpetrated the appalling acts of carnage and destruction but, more importantly, those who directed or inspired them – they would immediately constitute, in the eyes of most, an irrefutable confirmation of the dangerous naïveté of the person-centred view of human nature. To suggest even more outrageously that they, too, are infinitely beloved by the source of all being would constitute a scandalous affront to most conventional understandings of the divine dispensation.

In Chapter 2, I struggled with the conundrum of the personality of Adolf Hitler and came to no conclusion. That he embodied evil remains indisputable and even if, as I postulated, the permanent rejection of his own loving goes some way towards understanding his virulent hatred of much of the human race, it does not even begin to explain the monstrous atrocities which such hatred unleashed. It is perhaps more profitable to ponder whether this aberration of a human being was the result of the existence of a world which made such grotesque psychological deformity possible and then provided a ready arena for the implementation of its violent and sick agenda. Could it be that without a First World War, the Treaty of Versailles, the world recession, massive unemployment and – perhaps most significant of all – a deep sense in Germany of national inferiority and worthlessness, Adolf Hitler would have been a mere footnote in the history books and perhaps not even that?

Such speculation is not irrelevant as the world trembles on the verge of we know not what. It challenges the person-centred therapist to attempt the unthinkable and to enter empathically the mind of the terrorist and to consider the nature of the world which has nurtured the deformed human psyches that perpetrated the atrocities of 11 September 2001. The targets themselves offer some clues. The terrorists chose to obliterate the twin towers of the World Trade Center – giant symbols of the financial and commercial global empire – and to attempt the destruction of the Pentagon – symbol of American military might. The hatred of economic and military superiority is clear, as is the single-minded and desperate determination to bring down the powerful. To enter the mind of the terrorist is to discover, perhaps, a perception of reality which is only possible for someone who has been humiliated, invalidated and deprived of all hope. The empathic tracking must, however, enter even more treacherous and sinister terrain for it is clear that terrorists, however much they may experience humiliation, invalidation and hopelessness, are inspired by a cause which is of greater importance than their own lives. They do not conceptualize themselves as evil but rather as single-minded martyrs in the service of right. Indeed, it may well be that only such a cause can hold the promise of restoring a sense of dignity and self-respect to those who have experienced, either directly or vicariously, humiliation, abuse and exclusion from not only the so-called good things of life but from the very basic resources that make life tolerable at all. There is in the mind and heart of the terrorist an implacable rage which rails against what is experienced as gross injustice, and therein lie the seeds of the madness. It is a rage which attempts in vain to remedy the sense of communal worthlessness by destroying the power which has induced the self-denigration and shame in the first place.

It is, of course, possible that this empathic tracking of the terrorist's mind is wide of the mark in one significant respect. A sense of injustice and of rage can be induced not by economic disadvantage or material poverty but by a psychological fury at the pre-eminence of a philosophy and a way of life which are deemed to be wrong and demonic. It would seem that some of the leading suspects in the hunt for the perpetrators of the terrorist atrocities of 11 September are in no way the victims of material deprivation and economic injustice. On the contrary they have benefited from the material and cultural benefits of the Western consumerist and competitive culture. Such apparent benefits, however, may not have reduced the sense of shame and anger at having profited from a false ideology and its world of materialist greed and ethical double-think. Self-contempt can be the outcome of one's own behaviour as well as the result of denigration by others. Should this be the case, then in the terrorist's mind the only hope of self-respect will be in the attempted destruction of the ideology which has been the vehicle for self-betrayal, and what better process than to use the very money which has accrued from the collusion with false gods? Perhaps the motivation is a sinister mixture of shame and zeal and the 'war', if war it is, is truly the outcome of a religious and cultural collision which only the deepest empathy can hope to understand, let alone begin to heal.

Wherever the roots lie, however, the rage is inspired by self-disgust masquerading as heroic courage, and as such it merely adds horrifically to the sum total of human misery and threatens to unleash a response which will hasten a global madness where all respect for human life disappears. Self-contempt engenders violence and the desire to destroy. It may cloak itself in the mantle of a religious mission or in the rhetoric of a crusading right to revenge and retribution. The end result will be the same – a catastrophic retreat from the challenge of what it means to be fully human and from the creation of a world where the infinite worth of every unique individual and his or her desire to love and to be loved constitute the absolute and unshakeable principles for all human conduct and every human community. There are those rare occasions when we perhaps glimpse the faint possibility of such a world – in a group, for example, where cultural and racial distinctions are celebrated rather than feared or in those unforgettable moments when two persons are swept up in mutual and intense delight in each other's being. Then it becomes blindingly evident that we are members one of another and that when one suffers all suffer. In such moments, too, we know that the earth is our common home and that to desecrate it is to collude with our own destruction.

I do not know if this book will ever be published, so great is the uncertainty which currently confronts us all. If it appears as planned in 2002 it will assuredly be to a world that is much changed. My hope is that a global conflict will have been averted and that humanity will have seized the opportunity to face the rift in our collective soul and to begin on the long road to healing. My fear, of course, is that we shall have succumbed to the age-long curse of an eye for an eye and a tooth for a tooth and a limb for a limb so that, in the grim words of Deepak Chopra's current internet letter, we are left 'blind, toothless and crippled' (Chopra 2001).

It is my conviction, however, that good can come out of the darkest evil, as my fellow citizen, Julian, taught 600 years ago. My purpose in writing this book is to claim for person-centred therapy a role in this transformational process. Such a claim may seem outrageous and there have been times when I have been close to abandoning the whole project in order to avoid the incredulity or, worse, the pity of my fellow therapists. I know only too well that there is plenty to incite such a contemptuous response. I have claimed that person-centred therapy, with its steadfast belief in the resourcefulness of the person and in the power of the facilitative environment, gives access to an intensity of meeting which makes possible for individuals the profound realization of their own belovedness. Such knowledge in turn releases healing energy in therapist and client which finds both accompaniment and confirmation in the benevolent forces of the invisible world.

Such a claim is grandiose enough, but I go further and suggest that there comes from the practice of this therapeutic approach the experiential knowledge which can help bridge the divide between science and religion, create dialogue between the great world faiths and save the ravaged earth from final destruction. Whatever the aftermath of the fateful events of 11 September 2001, the world will surely have need of such a hope and of the means for realizing it in the face, perhaps, of the darkest despair. The profound gift of person-centred therapy is that it offers to every person an affirmation of being and a way of approaching the unknown other which promises liberating encounter rather than hostile suspicion. It is a mystical path which requires no dogma and no temple other than the human heart. What is more, it can banish shame and guilt because it acknowledges vulnerability and woundedness as the precursors of hope rather than as the signs of weakness and defeat.

When Carl Rogers wrote to his friends in March 1986 at the end of his courageous tour of a South Africa still in the grips of apartheid, he could say with passion:

> I will end with one conviction which grows out of all this experience. Violence *could* be avoided. No group really *wants* violence. If it could be brought about that there would be a prolonged, facilitated, person-to-person meeting of *all* the real leaders of the different major groups (including, of course, Nelson Mandela, who has been jailed for more than 20 years), I am convinced that a reasonably peaceful solution would be found.
>
> (Rogers 1986)

Deepak Chopra concludes his internet message with words which resonate powerfully with Rogers' conviction that, in the case of South Africa, proved so marvellously prophetic:

If you and I are having a single thought of violence or hatred against anyone in the world at this moment, we are contributing to the wounding of the world.

(Chopra 2001)

It is my belief that those who commit themselves to the mystical path which person-centred therapy illuminates can assuredly contribute to the healing of the nations and to the evolution of a world where violence is no more. The only question is whether we have already reached the point of no return. The hope that lies beyond despair continues to whisper passionately that it is not so.

Appendix

The following commentary on an interview is taken, with the permission of author and publisher, from *Living in Godless Times* by Alison Leonard, published by Floris Books of Edinburgh (2001).

A secular priest?

Brian Thorne was born in 1937, the only child of a butcher's assistant in Bristol. From 1974 until his semi-retirement in 1997 he was Director of Counselling at the University of East Anglia in Norwich, where he continues as director of the Centre for Counselling Studies. He co-founded the Norwich Centre, committed to the person-centred approach to therapy of Carl Rogers, and has written much on this theme including a study of Rogers' life and work.[1] He also holds appointments in Paris and Vienna. A member of the Church of England, he has offered mediation and group facilitation to the church in conflict situations. He is currently Lay Chairman of the Bishop's Council in the Diocese of Norwich.

I meet Brian in the Norwich Centre and he warns me at the beginning of our talk that he might not be very lively because he has just suffered the death of his step-mother Daisy. His grief for her is great, because not only did she marry his father four years before his death, she was midwife at Brian's birth, cared for him for the first six months of his life and was present throughout his childhood. It is part of an extraordinary story.

"In some strange way that I've not always been conscious of, there has been a sense of danger around in my life. My mother had rheumatic fever as a young woman, and it left her heart so badly impaired that she was told she would never have children." *So he was born against the odds? She was willing to face the danger?* "Yes. And so was my father. I imagine it wasn't an altogether joyous time for me in the womb, and I decided to get out early, by about a month. My mother had had an appallingly difficult labour and went into what we would now call a post-natal depression. I was not only premature but very sickly.

95

"But though there was a lot of danger around – something of a leitmotif in my life – there was also the necessary help there." *His step-mother?* "Daisy was my mother's best friend. She also delivered me, she gave me maternal care during my mother's illness, and she became my godmother. It must have been a strange experience for my father. He was a very quiet man, a man of tremendous fidelity, equilibrious, always responsive in a generous way to those who came into the butcher's shop. Someone approached me after my father's funeral and said, 'You do know, don't you, that your father kept many of us going during the war?'. He was such a symbol of strength and serenity, she said, he always smiled, and some people would go into the shop simply to exchange the time of day with him." *I suggest that there is something almost angelic in that, and Brian agrees.* "He played with me, cricket and table football. He was deeply involved in dealing with me in those early years."

Preserved from danger

The theme of being at risk and yet being cared for was strongly reflected in Brian's childhood experiences during the war. Does he interpret this theme in terms of God? "I do. I feel I have been preserved, I presume because it is important that I continue to exist. I have had a sense of vocation, at times very clear, at other times not so clear: I have been preserved in order to respond to my calling. It's only in the last twenty-odd years that I have reflected on these things and begun to make some sense of them.

"The first time that the Luftwaffe bombed Bristol was a Sunday night, and my mother and father and I were visiting my father's mother on the other side of Bristol. I was only three years old, but I'm sure the memory is mine, not a story told to me. Just as we were preparing to leave, the siren went and we had to go down and cower in her cellar. There was an incredible crash from above, and I remember my grandmother – an alarming woman, of whom I was frightened – shouting 'What's that?' and going upstairs and coming back down with an enormous piece of shrapnel that had come through the glass roof of the kitchen. It was almost beautiful, a big silver creation. Anyone in the way of it would have surely been killed. The all-clear didn't go for hours, till about 2 o'clock in the morning. Then we walked home through a city ablaze. I remember feeling more and more tired, and my father had to carry me. Because we were all so tired we decided to go to my mother's parents' house, which was about a mile nearer. I remember that Holy Nativity Church, Knowle – a church that for me was to become very important – was in flames. And I also remember, as we climbed the hill, how difficult it was to walk because the sweet shop at the top had been bombed, and all the stickiness was trickling down the hill, so it was like walking through glue. Then we turned the corner into the street where my grandparents lived and found, not a house, but a hole. The remains of a piano was hanging from the wall."

His grandparents were killed? "No, but I remember my mother screaming and fainting, and the neighbours running out and plying her with brandy and saying, 'It's all right, they went to the air-raid shelter,' which had only been completed the week before. Terrible danger, so close. But it was all right."

Did the rest of the family have a sense of being saved by God? "I don't recollect any expression of that feeling. But I feel sure that would have been the interpretation of my uncle, my mother's brother, who was also in the air-raid shelter. He was a church organist and devout Christian."

I point out that he had mentioned "war-time experiences", in the plural. "Oh yes. There was another. It was in 1942 or 1943. My mother and I were out shopping and we were waiting for the bus. The bus came, and we had that tiresome experience of climbing on the bus and then being shoved off again because it was too full. As soon as the bus crawled away the siren went, and five minutes later that bus suffered a direct hit."

That's very scary. Has he ever suffered from what they call "survivor's guilt"? "No. But I have felt survivor's *responsibility*." *Quite a weight to bear?* "Yes. And sometimes I feel I've been deluded." *Felt that it might just be chance?* "Well, I try to think that. But it doesn't last more than five minutes. Which is tiresome, because I don't want to be that important."

Does he ever think, "You're an arrogant bastard"?

"Yes. Am I just a pontificator, am I suffering from a *folie de grandeur?* When I was about sixteen I went to see a Franciscan friar who was visiting my school, and I remember saying to him – as passionate adolescents are wont to do – 'I think I'm meant to serve God but I don't quite know how,' and him saying, 'Well you'd better go back and get on with your French prose, hadn't you.'" Brian laughs. "And later in the same conversation he said, 'The trouble with you, I suspect, is not that you're arrogant, but that you're fearful you'll be seen as arrogant.' Very perceptive, and also very helpful."

There are other war stories, too. He was evacuated out of Bristol to two different places in the countryside, and on each occasion Bristol was completely air-raid free; then, on the evening he was brought back, all hell was let loose. So his parents gave up and kept him at home.

The pivotal experience of God

But he wasn't Mummy's little boy. His mother was naturally protective of him, but he resisted this. "I told her after she had collected me from school on my first day that she must never come to meet me again. She was terribly distressed. I was upset that she was upset, but at the same time I knew that I mustn't give way. Later I did relent on one issue: I consented to go to Clifton College on a scholarship rather than go with my mates to the state grammar school, because my saying No was causing her so much pain. It was good for my education, I think, that I did.

"My other memory of infants school is of the siren going and me sitting in the air-raid shelter telling stories to entertain the other children. I also invented a quite complicated language so that I could have secret conversations with a six-year-old girl called Pauline who I'd fallen heavily for. I wasn't lonely, though I did feel different from other children." *Why was that?* "I think partly because of the difference in intelligence, but partly because of what I now know is an empathic capacity, an ability to know what is going on in other people's minds. That was a source of great joy, but also of great pain. I picked up all sorts of things that I couldn't at the time understand."

Brian's mother was a fine singer, and with her brother also being an organist the house was full of music. He tells movingly of the last time his mother sang in public, and then says: "Now. That brings us up to what happened to me in 1946. It was the pivotal experience of my life. I've written about it, and I'll recount it again to try and give it some sort of shape.

"I'd started going to church. My mother went occasionally, my father not at all. An old lady who lived in the road asked if I'd like to go to church with her, a high Anglican church, the daughter church of the Holy Nativity. My parents agreed, and off I went. And I was hooked." *Was this G-O-D, or the music, or the drama, or what? Brian ponders.* "It was the immediate recognition," he says carefully, "that I'd stumbled into something that was of supreme importance." *And how old was he?* "I was seven or eight.

"I don't remember being 'close to God' as such. What I do remember is that in that church I could be really alive". *In what way?* "So many of my senses were being satisfied: the music, the beautiful flowers, the well-ordered liturgy, the colours, the vestments, the singing. And what's more, these young priests – there were four curates – preached sermons that I could *understand*!

"Then came the event. Good Friday 1946. I was nine. I was playing cricket in the park – I remember it was full of air-raid shelters with their roofs blown off – when suddenly, round a bend in the road came a religious procession, a Procession of Witness, from my church. Incense, the choir, the congregation behind . . . I'm not entirely sure what was going on inside me, but what I do know is that I was completely overwhelmed, and I ran home. I just ran. Went up to my bedroom, and sobbed and sobbed and sobbed. I don't know for how long. All I know is that from that day onwards I knew that I was infinitely loved.

"I knew it almost in the articulated way that I'm now talking about it. If God was like this (for now I was articulating it as a 'God thing') then it was all right to be playing cricket on Good Friday. 'No matter what people tell you, you're all right. Don't ever forget that.'

How did those words come? Did they come this way (I put my hands inwards) or that way (outwards)? "I'm not sure. The psychotherapist in me would like to say they came this way" (inwards) "but I don't think they did, I think they came that way" (outwards). "Whatever was happening came from An Other. Completely. No question."

Did he tell anyone? "No. Not until years and years later. But it changed my life."

Commitment to the church, openness to the other

"My commitment to the church became absolute. My parents must have thought it was a bit odd, but they didn't stop me. The church was wonderful. By the time I was ten I became a friend of Father Gerard Irvine, who was the first of many significant priests in my life. He was eccentric, a brilliant young man, a poet, with a lot of friends in high places. Through him I met John Betjeman and Stevie Smith. He took a great fancy to me." *Of course these days, I point out, we would ask, "What sort of a fancy was that?"* "Indeed. But Father Irvine was devoted to the notion of celibacy. He related to me as an adult, which was what I needed. He took me to the theatre, he came to the school and took part in the Fathers' Race – 'I'm Father to everyone!' he said. My parents loved him, he was so outrageous and so loving. The other priests, including the vicar, were also very good to me."

At the age of eleven, off went Brian the butcher's assistant's boy to Bristol's premier academic "public" school, Clifton. "It was very lonely. Fortunately I've always been good at languages, so I very quickly changed my accent from Bristolian to BBC.

"I also stayed very close to God. One thing I was quite sure of was that whatever other changes were taking place in my life, my devotion to God and to Holy Nativity Church were not going to change."

That was extraordinarily purposeful for a boy of eleven, wasn't it? "I wasn't conscious of that at the time. I just felt there were things I had to do, even though I might want to do them and *not* want to do them, both at the same time. I also found out what 'false religion' was. They had it at school. I had the real thing at Holy Nativity.

"Then there was another priest, Stuart Tayler, who became an enormous friend to me and to my family. When I was seventeen Stuart took me for the first of many times as his travelling companion to Greece and Italy, and opened up their treasures to me. My organist uncle who died young had left me some money which he stipulated could only be spent on foreign travel; he'd never been out of Britain and could have had no idea that I would study foreign languages. But it meant that I could go abroad and do a sort of Grand Tour."

At this point I ask Brian whether entry into a monastic community was ever a possibility for him. He hesitates before replying. "No. I don't think it was, but yes, there has always been in me a tension between being in the world and wanting to be apart from the world. There's a resentment sometimes that the 'apartness' gets a very small portion of my time. The yearning for it is now coming back quite strongly."

Did he ever want to go into the priesthood?

"Yes, but that was scotched very easily. I decided that I'd wear a priest's 'dog collar' when I was travelling from Bristol Temple Meads to Paddington, and just see what happened. I had a compartment to myself the whole way." *So the love of God was not to be transmitted that way?* "No. But at the same time, here were these phenomenal priests who were transmitting the love of God to me.

"I must mention my National Service.* That was terribly important. My basic training taught me not to be a physical coward. Then I went to Cyprus as an infantry officer. In the Officers' Mess were some of my mates from Clifton, and in the ranks were some of my mates from primary school." *Was that a problem?* "I didn't find it a problem. But there were some really significant events here".

We're back to the danger theme again. "The first was when we were driving along and out comes a terrorist and throws a bomb in front of the jeep. I shout 'Drive on!' and we go over the top of it – and it doesn't explode.

"The other one, we're driving down in a three-ton truck from the Troodos Mountains, the whole platoon in the back, and the driver turns to me and says, 'Sir, the brakes have gone'. That driver managed somehow to get this three-tonner off the road and save our lives, running up a hill instead of over the edge." *I know the Troodos Mountains and their gorges. I can imagine it.*

I ask Brian if he had conversations with God at this time, particularly about the morality of the army's role. "I had terrible problems with my conscience over the British role in Cyprus. Particularly when I was guarding women in prison, young women who had been distributing anti-British propaganda. I would get the platoon out of the way and simply talk to them. And the compassion that *they* showed *me* was extraordinary.

"What was strengthened in me in Cyprus was my openness to different cultures and belief systems. I ended up writing to Archbishop Makarios after he became the first president of independent Cyprus, wishing him well from someone who had fought against 'his' men. He replied to my letter, and from then on I got a Christmas card from him almost every year until he died."

This openness to the "enemy" wasn't wholly new. "At Clifton I'd decided to study German – not a popular decision, one of my uncles who'd been in the army didn't speak to me for two years – and I'd been on an exchange to Hamburg and met a family where the father had fought and been killed on the Russian front. I felt very strongly about what had happened to them in the war. It was in the German language, when I was staying with that family in Hamburg, that I managed for the first time to say things from the heart. Clifton College had taught me how to say things from my head, but German taught me how to speak from my heart. I felt love for the younger son – I'm sure there was a homosexual tinge to that – and for the mother, for the whole family. I was able to tell them in their own language, and it was accepted. I was aware that this was also a profound spiritual experience."

A psychotherapy of love

After National Service he went to Cambridge. "It had become quite clear to me that I was to study and then teach modern languages, so that I could enable people to be more open to different influences and cultures. That decision had been taken many years before, actually, in a church in Italy.

"Then I went to Bristol University to do my teaching certificate. There my tutor was an extraordinary woman called Elizabeth Richardson, who pioneered the introduction of psychotherapeutic insights into the classroom. Throughout my year in Bristol I was a member of a 'sensitivity training group,' an outrageous thing to be doing right at the beginning of the sixties."

So how did his teaching career change into a career in psychotherapy? "My first school was Eastbourne College, which was changing from a traditional public school to one which was much more open to new and liberal influences. Boarding schools are filled with children with appalling stories to tell, and boys soon began to confide in me. I became a sort of amateur counsellor. The Head agreed, astonishingly, that I should follow some training at the Tavistock Institute of Human Relations, and in 1964 he actually agreed to my facilitating a sensitivity training group of sixth-formers where we explored what was going on for them, both personally and inter-personally." *Subversive!* "Yes. But supported by the Head.

"So then I had to decide which direction my career was going in. My decision-making was brought to a crunch when I was helping a boy who, looking back, must have been incipiently psychotic. Some of the staff were feeling I was getting too close to this boy, and in desperation I decided to ring up Finchden Manor, a therapeutic community in Kent for boys who had been written off by other people that was run by a remarkable man called George Lyward.[2] He answered the phone, and he invited me to come over, and George Lyward thereafter became one of the great influences in my psychotherapeutic career. He told me, 'You *are* this young man's therapist. Why don't you just get *on* with it?' So I did.

"George had the almost unique ability to relate to each person, with love, as they actually were. He was the only person I've ever known who could harness his anger creatively and lovingly. He was prepared to take enormous risks. I only learnt after his death that every time he did it he was afraid he was going to get it wrong. That taught me that to be a good therapist you don't always have to be secure. You work not from your strength but from your vulnerability."

Within the year he had married Christine, a house matron at Eastbourne College, and decided to retrain as a psychotherapist. Almost fortuitously he trained in the client-centred approach of Carl Rogers (as opposed to other approaches, such as psychodynamic or Gestalt) with which he was entirely at home. "It had tremendous trust in the human organism as essentially forward-moving, so long as an environment of facilitative conditions can be created. And those facilitative conditions are, first, empathy, with which I already knew I was both blessed and cursed; second, unconditional positive regard, and third, congruence, which means being properly in touch with what is going on in oneself and giving expression to it when appropriate. I realized that this was what in my untutored way I had been doing in my relationships so far. And I was enraptured with Carl Rogers' writing. His books are like having a conversation with him. There's a purity and profundity about them, and an immediate practical clinical application.

"Then I went into the student counselling service at Keele University. While I was there I wrote with colleagues the first British book on student counselling,[3] and put up with vilification from the psychiatric establishment who thought that no one should dabble in these things unless they'd had at least twenty-three years medical experience . . . Then I came to Norwich, where I've been ever since."

We have both been realizing, as we talk, what a high proportion has been concentrated on Brian's early experiences and how little on his subsequent highly successful and influential career. Not to mention how little spent on his work as a counsellor in sensitive situations of conflict in the Church of England, of which there have been high profile cases in recent years (though that of course is confidential). This is Brian's choice. All the more recent story has been a working out of the "God interventions" of his formative years.

I ask him now about Julian of Norwich,* whom he has called "a counsellor for our age".[4]

"She has been my spiritual guide for nearly forty years. I came to Norwich partly, I think, because it is her place. It seems to me that she was doing therapeutic work here six hundred years ago. She tells us that in God's eyes we are 'wondrous creatures', we are His darlings, we have within us all the properties of the God who made us. Yes, there is sin; we sin inevitably through our shame and grief, but it gives us a wonderful opportunity to be utterly child-like and vulnerable, and in this state to run to our mother God for immediate acceptance."

Family and absences

Family life is something I very much want to ask Brian about. I know that he is still married to Christine, and that he has three adult children. Have the pressures of his profession, and his involvement with the community of the church, meant that they have felt ignored? Brian laughs at the question, and explains that he's laughing because this is such an on-going issue for him.

"But, looking back, I had parents who trusted me to be intimately involved with others. My wife also trusts me to be intimately involved with others. As a therapist you're intimately involved with others all the time, behind closed doors. She copes with me being available to other people all the time. She not only accepts that, but makes it possible. She trusts that I will do that honourably."

And his children? Was he an absent father? "Well, I have asked them, and they tell me that was not their experience. I was sometimes missing, but when I was there I was really there. Their memories, they say, are full of my presence. One of the tremendous aspects of my step-mother's funeral was all of us being together, walking behind the coffin, and then all being together afterwards, totally relaxed and open with each other."

The church, and angels

What about his on-going relationship with the Church of England? He is a very prominent lay Anglican. Have there been any problems with the clergy?

"Many profound friendships," *he replies,* "but also some problems, yes. There has always been in the Anglican church a very powerful evangelical wing. Their theology I find extremely distasteful, because it seems to disregard the saving grace of the crucifixion and resurrection and to treat people as if they're still grievously in a state of original sin. As if they still need to be shown how vile they are before they can be saved." *Whereas having himself experienced the reverse, the unconditional love of God . . .* "Yes. I know we don't need to grovel. So that theology is so abhorrent to me, and in my life as a therapist I have so often had to relate to people who have been so badly damaged by it, that at times I feel unspeakably angry, and I have to be very careful with that anger. There's another strand too. There are clergy who, even though they may not altogether be conscious of it, are actually on a power trip. When they're on a power trip they can do all sorts of damaging things. And if it turns their priesthood into a power-seeking, career-climbing, ambitious affair, that can be disastrous. If I've been called in to try and sort out some church mess, it is quite often a mixture of these two things: a combination of the degrading of humanity and the lust for power, which results in a sort of malevolent narcissism. It's often intractable, because self-awareness would bring unbearable guilt and might actually lead to self-destruction. The evil must always be *out there* rather than *in here*.

"At times, involvement in these things has made me not want to be in this institution at all any longer. So I retreat, for the sake of my own healing".

At this point I ask Brian about his relationship with his own power, as a professor, as a churchman and as a therapist. "It's always a temptation. It's the most awful question for me." *He takes a deep breath.* "Going back to that experience in the park, from which the message for me was, 'All that really matters is being loved and loving.' Most people who come to the therapist's door are hurting, feeling unloved, often quite denigrated, that they are worthless. So the question is, how do you make them feel that they are lovable and have the capacity to love?

"That process seems to involve, at times, taking the most outrageous risks. In any relationship there is always the possibility that what you feel is a loving impulse may be interpreted by the other person as a power impulse. That what you really want is to have this person somehow as an extension of yourself. And when you move into a real depth relationship with a person, it is very difficult to have sufficient awareness to see what's going on. And even if that awareness is vouchsafed to you, you never truly know how the other person is going to experience it. What they experience as loving this year, they may next year interpret as power.

"As a therapist you should always explore these things with your supervisor, if they're the right sort of person. But it's at these points that God is absolutely essential to me. It means that somehow I have to try and stay as close as I possibly can to God, so that the possibility of my inadvertently succumbing to the power impulse is minimized. If I am out of touch with God, if I can't feel in contact with God, then I am in great danger, and my client is in great danger.

"Having said that, there is no way you can be a therapist without experiencing continual self-doubt. Back to George Lyward, who constantly suffered from self-doubt, and yet was a genius. I follow that path, and I never know from one day to the next whether I might fall into the pit. There have been times, in fact, when I *have* fallen into the pit. And I have been badly abused by clients, too. When either of these situations occurs, it is very tempting to give up. And it's at these times when it is vital to stay close to God and to Jesus in His Passion."

How does he do this? Stay close to God and to Jesus in His Passion?
"There are two fundamental things, as far as I'm concerned. One is the Eucharist. I don't know what I would do if I didn't have access to the Eucharist for any length of time. It enables me, usually, to feel that closeness to God, a kind of internalization of God, a taking of the divine into me, that is absolutely critical.

"The other thing is the attempt to see in other people that which is of Christ. That is a minute-by-minute discipline. It is the perception of God within others. It also ensures that I am nourished by the food of angels."

So, I suggest, his work is to access, by means of his own nature, the divine nature of others. "Yes. I never suggest any such theology to them, but I feel they are seeking it, whether they know it or not".

Sometimes he feels it is all too much. "I ask God, 'Why have you given me this terrible job, which is trying to love people into being? It's insufferably difficult, impossible. Why can't I have a safer orientation, be psychodynamic and retreat behind transference, be a behaviourist and just take people through behavioural exercises? Why *this* orientation, which depends wholly on the relationship and environment of loving between therapist and client? Why must I always face the possibility of doing something dreadful, of taking a risk which can turn out to be a potentially lethal risk?"

Does he retreat into the wilderness sometimes? "Not as often as I should. But I do have a facility to cut off. So I can move from one situation to another and leave things behind. Writing, too, is immensely satisfying."

Is there a spiritual movement in him through the medium of words? "Yes, there is. I'm nourished by poets, dramatists and novelists. In my study of languages I became steeped in the works of Goethe, for instance, and the seventeenth century dramatists, particularly Racine, and then there's Wordsworth. There is a sense in which I commune with writers at a spiritual level. I sense a whole company of witnesses. Angels and archangels. When I pass out of this body, that is the company I shall join."

Has he ever seen or felt angels? There seems to be something of an angelic trail through his life. "On a couple of occasions I have heard angelic voices. One was when I was in the middle of an appallingly difficult workshop for therapists, and I heard the most extraordinary singing. No one else heard it. And I knew it would be all right. After all, if these beings were so jubilant what the hell were we worrying about?

"The other occasion was in Lincoln Minster. I was staying with the Chapter Clerk, and we'd had a number of whiskies, and about one o'clock in the morning he said, 'Would you like to go over to the Minster?'. So we went over and turned off all the alarms and went into this amazing building, in the dark. At that time there'd been a lot of problems and someone had suggested that the Minster was evil. It wasn't even spooky or frightening. It was so friendly. A gentle monster. And that was the second time I heard singing. Whether it was the whisky or not I can't tell, but we both came out knowing that this was not where evil resided. I think they were angels singing."

Where are the angels in times and places where evil seems rampant? "The only answer I can offer is that the angels of God are in the pain. In the pain of those who commit the atrocities as much as in the pain of those who suffer."

At the moment, in his grief, Brian is looking into something of a mist as far as his life as a therapist and therapy trainer is concerned. "I'm unsure of my direction. But I know that I must wait. On George Lyward's wall there hung a poem by Richard Church that begins:

> Learning to wait consumes my life,
> consumes and feeds as well …

It's not always easy to wait, or to know when the waiting must end."

Notes

[1] See *Person-Centred Therapy Today* and *Carl Rogers,* both Sage publications, London.
[2] See *Mr Lyward's Answer,* by Michael Burn, Hamish Hamilton, London, 1956.
[3] *Student Counselling in Practice,* co-authored with Audrey Newsome and Keith Wyld, University of London Press, 1973.
[4] In *Julian of Norwich,* pamphlet published by the Guild of Pastoral Psychology, 1999.
[*] British military service, which was abolished in 1963.
[#] Anchoress and mystic who lived 1342-c1416, author of *Revelations of Divine Love,* a document of religious experience.

References

Baldwin M (ed.) (2000) The Use of Self in Therapy, 2nd edn. New York: The Haworth Press.

Barrett-Lennard G (1998) Carl Rogers' Helping System: Journey and Substance. London: Sage.

Bergin A (1991) Values and religious issues in psychotherapy and mental health. American Psychologist 46(4): 394–403.

Biermann-Ratjen E-M (1998) On the development of the person in relationships. In Thorne B, Lambers E (eds), Person-centred Therapy: a European Perspective. London: Sage. pp 106–18.

Binder U (1998) Empathy and empathy development with psychotic clients. In Thorne B, Lambers E (eds), Person-centred Therapy: a European Perspective. London: Sage. pp 216–30.

Bowen M (1986) Intuition in Psychotherapy. Unpublished paper.

BACP (2001) Ethical Framework for Good Practice in Counselling and Psychotherapy. Rugby: BACP.

Burn M (1956) Mr Lyward's Answer. London: Hamish Hamilton.

Chopra D (2001) Letter on the Internet, 12 Sep.

Frick WB (2000) Remembering Maslow: reflections on a 1968 interview. Journal of Humanistic Psychology 40(2): 128–47.

Gendlin ET (1978) Focusing. New York: Everest House.

Girard R (1996) The Girard Reader (ed. JG Williams). New York: Crossroad Publishing Company.

Griffiths B (1989) A New Vision of Reality. London: Fount.

Kirschenbaum H (1979) On Becoming Carl Rogers. New York: Delacorte Press.

Kübler-Ross E (1997) The Wheel of Life. London: Bantam Books.

Leonard A (2001) Living in Godless Times. Edinburgh: Floris Books.

Mearns D, Thorne B (1988) Person-Centred Counselling in Action. London: Sage.

Mearns D, Thorne B (1999) Person-Centred Counselling in Action, 2nd edn. London: Sage.

Mearns D, Thorne B (2000) Person-centred Therapy Today: New Frontiers in Theory and Practice. London: Sage.

Morotomi Y (1998) Person-centred counselling from the viewpoint of Japanese spirituality. Person-Centred Practice 6(1): 28–32.

Natiello P (2001) The Person-centred Approach: A Passionate Presence. Ross-on-Wye: PCCS Books.

Newsome A, Thorne B, Wyld K (1973) Student Counselling in Practice. London: University of London Press.

O'Leary C (1999) Counselling Couples and Families. London: Sage.

Owen Jones P (2000) Small Boat, Big Sea. Oxford: Lion.

Rogers CR (1959) A theory of therapy, personality and interpersonal relationships as developed in the client-centered framework. In Koch S (ed.), Psychology: A Study of Science, Vol. 3. Formulations of the Person and the Social Contract. New York: McGraw-Hill. pp 194–256.

Rogers CR (1975) The formative tendency. Paper presented at the Theory Conference of the Association for Humanistic Psychology, April 5.

Rogers CR (1978) The formative tendency. Journal of Humanistic Psychology 18(1): 23–26.

Rogers CR (1980) A Way of Being. Boston: Houghton Mifflin.

Rogers CR (1986) Journal of South African Trip, January 14–March 1, 1986. Unpublished paper.

Rogers CR (1995) What understanding and acceptance mean to me. Journal of Humanistic Psychology 35(4): 7–22.

Rosenbaum R (ed.) (1998) Explaining Hitler: The Search for the Origins of his Evil. London: Macmillan.

Thorne B (1989) The blessing and the curse of empathy. In Dryden W, Spurling L (eds), On Becoming a Psychotherapist. London: Tavistock/Routledge. pp 53–68.

Thorne B (1991) Person-centred Counselling: Therapeutic and Spiritual Dimensions. London: Whurr Publishers.

Thorne B (1992) Carl Rogers. London: Sage.

Thorne B (1997) Counselling and psychotherapy: the sickness and the prognosis. In Palmer S, Varma V (eds), The Future of Counselling and Psychotherapy. London: Sage. pp 153–66.

Thorne B (1999) Julian of Norwich. London: Guild of Pastoral Psychology.

Tomoda F (ed.) (1967) Kaunseringu no Gijutsu. Complete Works of Carl Rogers, vol. 8. Iwasaki Gakujutsu Shippan.

Vallély P (2001) A silent world, united in grief. The Independent, 15 September: 1.

van Kalmthout M (2000) The farther reaches of psychotherapy. Paper presented at the Fifth International Conference on Client-centered and Experiential Psychotherapy, Chicago, June.

White R (1997) Exceptional human experiences and the experiential paradigm. In Tart CT (ed.), Body, Mind, Spirit. Charlottesville, VA: Hampton Roads Publishing Company. pp 83–100.

Wilber K (1998) The Marriage of Sense and Soul: Integrating Science and Religion. Dublin: Newleaf.

Index